Building Your Library
Career with Web 2.0

DISCARDED FROM STOCK

CHANDOS

INFORMATION PROFESSIONAL SERIES

Series Editor: Ruth Rikowski
(e-mail: Rikowskigr@aol.com)

Chandos' new series of books is aimed at the busy information professional. They have been specially commissioned to provide the reader with an authoritative view of current thinking. They are designed to provide easy-to-read and (most importantly) practical coverage of topics that are of interest to librarians and other information professionals. If you would like a full listing of current and forthcoming titles, please visit our website www.chandospublishing.com or e-mail wp@woodheadpublishing.com or telephone +44 (0) 1223 499140.

New authors: we are always pleased to receive ideas for new titles; if you would like to write a book for Chandos, please contact Dr Glyn Jones on e-mail gjones@chandospublishing.com or telephone number +44 (0) 1993 848726.

Bulk orders: some organisations buy a number of copies of our books. If you are interested in doing this, we would be pleased to discuss a discount. Please contact on e-mail wp@woodheadpublishing.com or telephone +44 (0) 1223 499140.

Building Your Library Career with Web 2.0

JULIA GROSS

CP

CHANDOS
PUBLISHING

Oxford Cambridge New Delhi

STAFFORDSHIRE
UNIVERSITY
LIBRARY

2 8 JUN 2013

SITE: THOMPSON

CLASS NO. 020.23

Chandos Publishing
Hexagon House
Avenue 4
Station Lane
Witney
Oxford OX28 4BN
UK
Tel: +44 (0) 1993 848726
E-mail: info@chandospublishing.com
www.chandospublishing.com

Chandos Publishing is an imprint of Woodhead Publishing Limited

Woodhead Publishing Limited
80 High Street
Sawston
Cambridge CB22 3HJ
UK
Tel: +44 (0) 1223 499140
Fax: +44 (0) 1223 832819
www.woodheadpublishing.com

First published 2012

ISBN: 978-1-84334-651-7 (print)
ISBN: 978-1-78603-289-6 (online)

© J. Gross, 2012

British Library Cataloguing-in-Publication Data
A catalogue record for this book is available from the British Library.

All rights reserved. No part of this publication may be reproduced, stored in or introduced into a retrieval system, or transmitted, in any form, or by any means (electronic, mechanical, photocopying, recording or otherwise) without the prior written permission of the Publisher. This publication may not be lent, resold, hired out or otherwise disposed of by way of trade in any form of binding or cover other than that in which it is published without the prior consent of the Publisher. Any person who does any unauthorized act in relation to this publication may be liable to criminal prosecution and civil claims for damages.

The Publisher makes no representation, express or implied, with regard to the accuracy of the information contained in this publication and cannot accept any legal responsibility or liability for any errors or omissions.

The material contained in this publication constitutes general guidelines only and does not represent to be advice on any particular matter. No reader or purchaser should act on the basis of material contained in this publication without first taking professional advice appropriate to their particular circumstances. Any screenshots in this publication are the copyright of the website owner(s), unless indicated otherwise.

Typeset by RefineCatch Ltd, Bungay, Suffolk
Printed in the UK and USA.

Printed in the UK by 4edge Limited - www.4edge.co.uk

05803679

Contents

List of figures and tables

Figures

Tables

Preface

New LIS graduates, many of whom are of the so-called Net-generation, are pursuing their careers in a twenty-first-century fish-bowl, where the line between personal and work lives is starting to blur. I believe this book is timely, because not a day goes by without there being another media story about someone revealing too much personal information on a social networking site.

With my experience in staff training and development, and being a keen online social networker myself, I began to investigate how librarians utilise social networking for their careers. I was curious to find out how we participate in social networks and achieve a balance between our private and professional lives. Web 2.0 does pose a privacy threat, but it is not so great that it cannot be managed. And besides, for every threat there is a counter-balancing opportunity – Web 2.0 technologies can be used to build professional knowledge, to enhance networks and to develop a positive online presence.

This book is a result of my research into the use of Web 2.0 technologies by librarians as they pursue their career goals. I have explored the emerging literature about social networking and the library career and professional development literature. I have also tapped into my online personal learning networks to examine social networking among librarian practitioners.

My personal learning journey through some of the Web 2.0 technologies started with my being the joint project director of the Learning 2.0 program at Edith Cowan University Library in Perth, Western Australia. Learning 2.0 led me to starting blogging about emerging technologies in libraries and I have continued to record my learning about new Web 2.0 tools and to share my thoughts with colleagues and others.

When starting out to write this book, I decided that writing about the Web 2.0 technologies per se would be fraught with difficulties – it is a movable feast and the variety of tools and their mobile versions is daunting. Instead, the book is focused on the application of technologies to professional development, networking and marketing – the cornerstones of career development. The book includes chapters on social networking, marketing, privacy, lifelong learning, professional development, networking, mentoring and keeping up to date. For each chapter I have described a range of different technologies and applied them to each career area, thus providing an overall Web 2.0 career toolkit.

I trust all library and information professionals at any stage in their careers will find something for them in this book and that it will assist them to recognise and embrace the career development opportunities of emerging technologies in our increasingly networked world.

Acknowledgements

This book would not have been possible without the support of a number of people and institutions.

I wish to gratefully acknowledge the support of the Faculty of Education and Arts at Edith Cowan University in Perth, Western Australia. In particular my sincere thanks go to Professor Mark Hackling, Faculty Dean of Research, for extending support in the form of editorial services and participation in the faculty writing retreat. Some of the writing was done during the Faculty of Education and Arts Writing Retreat, facilitated by Dr Sally Knowles. My special thanks go to Sally, and to my fellow writers and colleagues at the retreat.

I also wish to sincerely thank Dr John Hall of Edith Cowan University for his wise editorial advice and critical feedback on the book.

And a special thanks to Mr Jonathan Davis, Dr Glyn Jones and the team at Chandos Publishing in Oxford, for guiding me through the book-writing process and helping to bring my project to fruition.

I thankfully acknowledge all my inspirational library colleagues and especially those on the online social networks and on my personal learning network, who may not have realised it, but their ideas contributed greatly.

And finally, my particular thanks go to Cathy and Peter for offering their bush retreat where I completed some of the writing. And thanks to all my family and especially my husband Wolf for his wonderful support and home cooking, and for helping me to find the time to complete the book.

March 2011
Building Your Library Career with Web 2.0
Julia Gross

About the author

Julia Gross is a faculty librarian at Edith Cowan University (ECU), in Perth, Western Australia. She graduated with a Bachelor of Arts degree from the University of Western Australia and a postgraduate degree in Librarianship from the University of New South Wales. Julia started her career in special and public libraries in Australia and Canada. For the past thirty years she has worked as an academic librarian, educator and manager, focusing on the areas of information services and faculty support.

Julia currently holds the position of Faculty Librarian for Education and Arts at ECU and manages a team of ten library and information professionals who provide library services to the faculty. In that role she is responsible for the team members' staff development, for the information literacy programmes, as well as collection management and development. Over many years Julia has developed particular skills in building partnerships with faculty and offshore institutions. She has been in the fortunate position of being involved in a range of university projects and partnerships.

From 2003 to 2004 Julia was the library consultant for a World Bank-funded Link Institution Project between the Maldives College of Higher Education and ECU. Since then she has continued to be active in mentoring librarians in the Indian Ocean region. During the years from 2001 to 2007 she travelled many times to Singapore as library ambassador, providing faculty library services and delivering information literacy programmes to cohorts of offshore students in Singapore.

In 2003 Julia was on the Western Australian Statewide Library Marketing Committee and was engaged in bringing the @ Your Library marketing campaign to the university libraries in Perth. At her own university she was responsible for implementing the library marketing campaign and fostering the development of a library marketing culture.

ECU was the first Australian university library to adopt the Learning 2.0 Programme (also known as the 23 Things) in 2007. Julia was joint project director of ECU Library Learning 2.0 and through the programme introduced Web 2.0 technologies to library staff. Subsequently, as well as being a faculty library manager, she has worked with staff on their continuing professional development in Web 2.0 technologies. She also led a joint faculty project on podcasting and played a vital role in producing library podcasts and embedding audio and video media within education courses in the faculty.

Over the past six months Julia has been endeavouring to re-invent herself as her institution's research data management expert. She is working on a national research data management project – the Seeding the Commons project, on behalf of the Australian National Data Service (ANDS) and ECU. This project is part of a national initiative to build the Australian Research Data Commons, a cohesive collection of Australian research resources from all research institutions across the nation.

Over the past ten years Julia has published on subjects as wide-ranging as podcasting, blogging, Library 2.0, professional development of librarians, libraries in developing countries, information literacy, usability, Web scale discovery and user behaviour. She has presented at international conferences in India, Australia, New Zealand and Sri Lanka.

Julia has continued to be actively engaged in her own professional education and has completed postgraduate studies in Management and in Teaching (Higher Education). She is an associate member of ALIA (Australian Library and Information Association) and was the president (2002-03) of the ALIA Academic and Research Librarians group of Western Australia. She is also on the Australian committee of ASSA (Association for the Study of Australasia in Asia), an organisation that promotes Australian Studies in the Asian region through its publications and conferences. She has received various ECU institutional awards for leadership and teamwork and in 2009 was a member of the ECU library team awarded the Vice-Chancellor's Citation for Outstanding Contribution to Student Learning. Subsequently the same library team won the highly competitive national award – the Citation for Outstanding Contribution to Student Learning from the Australian Learning and Teaching Council (ALTC).

Julia has a long-standing interest in new technologies and the continuing professional development of librarians. She is an enthusiastic follower of the Web 2.0 social networks and can be found engaging with colleagues on many of the social networks that she describes in her book.

The author may be contacted at:

E-mail: j.gross@ecu.edu.au

Web 2.0 and your library career

Abstract: This chapter highlights the need for LIS professionals to adapt and grow in the rapidly changing world of work. The chapter provides an overview of how emerging technologies and Web 2.0 have shaped libraries and library careers. It describes how Web 2.0 is impacting on job searching and highlights the part played by Web 2.0 in library career development. The chapter identifies three cornerstones of career activities where Web 2.0 can be applied: marketing, networking and professional development. Finally, the chapter describes how the book is structured to provide a plan for implementing some of the Web 2.0 technologies for one's career.

Key words: career, Web 2.0, LIS professionals, librarians, emerging technologies, social networking.

To be successful as library and information services (LIS) professionals, we need to adapt to the rapidly changing world of work. At various stages in our careers we are involved in the search for a job, or otherwise need to prove our worth to a prospective employer. And even if we are happily working in a library position, we need to continue to develop our expertise and build our networks to remain employable in the competitive LIS market. This book introduces you to some of the Web 2.0 technologies, particularly the social networking technologies that are vital for your career development. These technologies can enhance your professional development and help you make your career future-proof. Keeping up with the profession is always crucial, especially during economically tough times, when fewer jobs may be on offer. The book gives you the contexts and some specific examples for using these Web 2.0 tools.

Web 2.0 technologies provide us with some tools to help build a career and maintain our professional edge. This book describes how these technologies relate to career development – to networking, lifelong learning, professional development and marketing. Specifically, the book provides you with a plan of action and a Web 2.0 toolkit to work with.

Prior to what can only be described as the revolutionary Web 2.0 technological changes, we approached job seeking and career growth and development with offline tools such as a resumé or curriculum vitae, a strategy to help us perform well in job interviews, and maybe a portfolio of evidence of our applicable skills, abilities and competencies. Now online connectivity and Web 2.0 has opened up new opportunities for us to network, learn and grow in our careers.

Technology and the core business of libraries

Libraries have always striven to connect people to information, resources and services. But our core business in the library and information services field has evolved from providing information to enabling literacy, and creating learning communities. Stephen Abram (leading international librarian and author of the *stephenslighthouse.com* blog) puts it like this: 'libraries core skill is not delivering information ... libraries are about learning and building communities' (2007). But to perform these roles effectively we need to adapt, grow, stay up to date and stay connected.

Our technological past and future

Technology is a key tool that enables librarians, as well as many other professionals, to perform their role, and it has been a component of LIS jobs since the latter half of the twentieth century.

As an academic librarian, I remember in the early 1990s, library professionals were raising awareness on campus among academic staff and students of the coming Internet revolution. Now, in the second decade of the twenty-first century, I work with academic colleagues in teaching and learning and information technology departments, to embed online technologies. And for the LIS profession at large, technology is more than ever a key mechanism for performing our roles.

When Web 2.0 was first talked about in the first decade of the twenty-first century it was seen by TALIS (Teaching and Learning International Survey) as a game-changing 'disruptive' innovation (Miller, 2006). However, many library professionals soon realised that these technologies were enabling tools that could help us to interact with our user communities and share our knowledge. By this time libraries were already involved in automating their operational functions and in providing online access to library digital collections. And this next generation of technologies – the Web 2.0 social technologies – were very much aligned with this evolution.

What is Web 2.0?

Although the term Web 2.0 is in popular use in the mainstream, it is a term that is somewhat contested. Since 2004, when Tim O'Reilly of O'Reilly Media first used the term, there have been many attempts to clarify what it means.

Initially, after the so-called 'dot com crash', Web 2.0 was used to describe new technologies that were different from the Web 1.0 developments of the previous decade. The term Web 2.0 in a broad sense refers to a group of softwares and websites that emphasise community building, online collaboration and social networking, where users interact online and create and shape online content. The concept is better understood when we actually work with these softwares. Some examples of the technologies that typify the change to Web 2.0 are: blogs, wikis, podcasts, social networking softwares, RSS feeds and feed readers (which push syndicated content out to users). In the Web 2.0 world everyone is able to add, edit and mash together content, activity that contributes to the creation of a socially networked web environment. So it was not so much the new technologies themselves, but how they were being used, that inspired the online community, from geeks to the average end users. Ideally, the technologies would be used to create a truly participatory culture that moved beyond usage patterns of the previous decade. One clear and dramatic example of Web 2.0 moving into the mainstream globally is the way political campaigners are using social media sites such as Twitter and Facebook to get their message out.

Clearly Web 2.0 revolutionises the way we look at and use the Internet, and it impacts on all aspects of career development, from job seeking, to career advancement, marketing, networking and professional development. These are the areas I will be focusing on in this book.

Why should LIS professionals be interested in Web 2.0?

As stated above, the way librarians find new job opportunities and build their careers has changed because the Web 2.0

social softwares, which were developed to enhance online interaction, have permeated organisational structures. In addition, the mainstreaming of Web 2.0 and social technologies means that we are all becoming visible online to a greater or lesser extent. This increased online visibility is both a threat and an opportunity.

Furthermore, Web 2.0 is starting to impact at the personal level. For example, our views on privacy are changing, with differences across generations, as will be discussed in Chapter 5. Social networking privacy concerns and the impact on employability are being covered in the mainstream media. As professionals it is imperative that we heed these concerns and guard our professional reputations. One positive aspect of social networking software is that we can use these tools to build networks, and market ourselves, and become better informed as professionals.

What are the key features of Web 2.0 that make it useful in careers?

Some compelling reasons for LIS professionals to embrace Web 2.0 are that it:

- encourages greater interaction and a sense of openness between professionals;
- enables professionals to share and change content (e.g. wikis, group documents, photos);
- lets professionals create personal profiles and build an online identity;
- enables professional communities to be created around a theme;
- facilitates collaborations and globalisation;

- encourages a breakdown of barriers across disciplines – convergence;
- breaks down barriers across organisational levels, leading to democratisation in the workplace;
- gives a competitive advantage to those who can effectively use the new Web 2.0 networks;
- speeds up communication;
- puts the power with the end-user as it provides simple and easy-to-use interfaces.

What are the risks and pitfalls of Web 2.0?

Throughout the book I will be touching on the downside of these technologies, particularly in relation to concerns for privacy. In many cases it will come down to finding a balance between the benefits of participation versus the risk to our privacy. Some specific risks for Web 2.0 are that it:

- blurs the lines between the private space and the public space;
- threatens privacy;
- increases the possibility of identity fraud, putting reputations at risk.

Web 2.0 and the workplace generally

Web 2.0 now permeates working lives within organisations. These new ways of doing things are affecting organisational communication and the workplace, leading to the emergence of the notion of an 'enterprise 2.0' where organisations use collaborative social networking communities.

The CCH white paper, *Professionals and Web 2.0* (2008), looked into the use of social networking within a wide range of professional groups, finding high usage of Web 2.0 both personally and professionally. Whereas this study did not target librarians or information workers specifically, it indicated increasing use among professionals (see Table 1.1) and this usage would have continued to increase in the past two years.

Table 1.1	CCH white paper on professionals and Web 2.0 (2008)

	Type of usage	Percentage of professionals
Web 2.0 usage as information source at least once a week	Overall usage	59
Web 2.0 usage as information source at least once a week	Work purposes usage	43.7

Furthermore, it is evident now that employees and employers are using Web 2.0 social networking sites for recruitment purposes. According to a CareerBuilder survey in June 2009, 45 per cent of employers used social networking sites such as Facebook to screen potential employees (Haefner and CareerBuilder, 2009). Additionally, 16 per cent of employees used such sites in the process of job seeking. This data is based on a survey of more than 2,600 hiring managers in the United States. The pattern of responses indicates that social networking sites are increasingly being used in recruitment. Anecdotal evidence from employers I have spoken to indicates that many would at least explore some online options, such as searching Google, to screen applicants in the recruitment process.

Employers who completed the CareerBuilder survey used the social networking sites below to screen job candidates:

- 29 per cent used Facebook;
- 26 per cent used LinkedIn;

- 21 per cent used MySpace;
- 11 per cent used a blog search;
- 7 per cent used Twitter.

Qualitative data from the CareerBuilder survey indicated that these employers made use of job candidates' online profiles on social networking sites in a variety of ways, as shown below:

- 50 per cent to see if the profile provided a good feel for the candidate's personality and fit within the organisation;
- 39 per cent to check whether the profile supported the candidate's professional qualifications;
- 38 per cent to see if the candidate was creative;
- 33 per cent to see if the candidate was well-rounded;
- 19 per cent to check whether other people posted good references about the candidate;
- 15 per cent to ascertain if the candidate had received awards and accolades.

Cornerstones of career development

The book will look at three cornerstones of career development: *marketing, networking* and *professional development.* The chapters are grouped around the cornerstone areas, looking at the Web 2.0 tools that can be applied to develop knowledge and competencies in each area. The first three chapters set the scene, develop the theme of Web 2.0 and social networking and look into current social networking sites. Then I move on to chapters related to marketing, networking and professional development. A brief synopsis of the three cornerstones and how the book is structured follows.

Marketing

Chapter 4 on marketing deals with your web presence and how you can use online profiles to develop your personal brand. I talk about how to build a positive online identity and some impediments to self promotion. In Chapter 5 I look at the critical issues surrounding privacy. In an online world, where many of us have a digital footprint, new rules apply. The chapter gives you practical advice on how to ensure privacy and protect your reputation online.

Learning and professional development

As stated above, if you are already in the workforce and working at your profession you are in a fortunate position. However, in competitive markets where organisational restructures and downsizings are rampant you never know what is around the corner. As LIS workers we need to remain relevant and employable. Chapters 6 and 7 are about lifelong learning and professional development. Chapter 10 is devoted to keeping up to date to maintain your competitive edge and having a good plan to cope with information overload.

Networking

The networking that used to take place within organisations and through professional organisations and societies has now been amplified with the emergence of social networking sites. Whereas the face-to-face meeting in formal and informal contexts is still a vital part of professional development, online relationships between trusted colleagues are becoming a special new feature in the Web 2.0 environment. Sites such as LinkedIn, Facebook and Twitter can help us communicate and connect to the wider world of international professionals at all levels and in related disciplines. In Chapter 9 I look at mentoring in the Web 2.0 environment, in particular how e-mentoring relationships can be strengthened and deepened through online social networks.

The book is structured around the three cornerstones of career development, rather than the specific technologies per se. The primary focus is on what needs to be done. How we do it, using the Web 2.0 technologies, is the secondary consideration. Web 2.0 technologies provide tools that we can harness to serve our overall purpose of career development. Table 1.2 below shows how the book is structured and how the chapters fit together.

As you can see from the table, the book includes chapters on *who you are*, on *who you know* and on *what you know*, all of which are vital concerns for career development.

Table 1.2 Structure of the book

	Structure of the book		
	Who you are	**Who you know**	**What you know**
Chapter	*Marketing*	*Networking*	*Professional development*
2	Social networking	Social networking	Social networking
3	Social networking sites		
4	Marketing		
5	Privacy		
6			Lifelong learning
7			Professional development
8		Networking	
9		Mentoring	
10			Keeping up to date

Conclusion

In the second decade of the twenty-first century, Web 2.0 has become part of the mainstream so it is time to take stock of its wider implications for LIS professionals. This book is about LIS career development in the Web 2.0 era: developing your online presence, staying relevant, and building networks to survive in the competitive marketplace. Getting a job, changing jobs, staying employable, keeping your job, future-proofing your career is more important than ever during tough economic times when fewer jobs may be on offer. For LIS professionals the evidence that employers are using social networking sites should be welcomed, as this provides opportunities to position ourselves advantageously.

The book is not a comprehensive library career guide; there are others in this series (such as Ptolomey's *Taking Charge of Your Career: A guide for the library and information professional*, De Stricker and Hurst-Wahl's *The Information and Knowledge Professional's Career Handbook: Define and create your success* and Heye's *Characteristics of the Successful Twenty-First-Century Information Professional*) that will help guide you along what is obviously a rapidly changing path for the development of a career in librarianship. The book does not offer any guarantees; it presents strategies in career development that I have found bring results. In closing this chapter, I feel obliged to alert you: as with all technology topics, the information in this book is not fixed and will change. Within the time of writing this book some well used Web 2.0 sites have closed down, namely Bloglines (the RSS feed reader), and some are under threat of sale or closure, namely Delicious (the social bookmarking site). But our line of business as information professionals is in keeping up with changing information, and the book will guide us on where to go to locate and validate new Web 2.0 sources.

References

Abram, S. (2007) *The Future of Libraries*. Retrieved 20 May 2008, from *http://stephenslighthouse.com/files/MontereyPL.pdf*.

CCH (2008) *Professionals and Web 2.0: Findings from the CCH White Paper and What it Means for Information Providers*. Retrieved 20 April 2010, from *http://www.cch.com.au/DocLibrary/cch_professionals_web20_whitepaper_final.pdf*.

Cook, N. (2008) *Enterprise 2.0: How Social Software Will Change the Future of Work*. Aldershot; Burlington, VT: Gower.

De Stricker, U. and Hurst-Wahl, J. (2011) *The Information and Knowledge Professional's Career Handbook: Define and Create Your Success*. Oxford: Chandos.

Haefner, R. and CareerBuilder (2009) *More Employers Screening Candidates via Social Networking Sites: Five Tips for Creating a Positive Online Image*. Retrieved 20 April 2010, from *http://msn.careerbuilder.com/Article/MSN-2035-Job-Info-and-Trends-More-Employers-Screening-Candidates-via-Social-Networking-Sites/*.

Heye, D. (2006) *Characteristics of the Successful Twenty-First-Century Information Professional*. Oxford: Chandos.

Maness, J.M. (2006) *Library 2.0 theory: Web 2.0 and its Implications for Libraries*. Webology, 3(2), Article 25. Retrieved 20 April 2010, from *http://www.webology.ir/2006/v3n2/a25.html*.

Miller, P. (2006) *Library 2.0: The Challenge of Disruptive Innovation. A TALIS White Paper*. Retrieved 4 March 2008, from *http://www.talis.com/tdn/node/1304*.

Ptolomey, J. (2009) *Taking Charge of Your Career: A Guide*

for the Library and Information Professional. Oxford: Chandos.

Useful weblink

Abram, Stephen *Stephen's Lighthouse* (blog): *http://stephens lighthouse.com/*

2

Social networking sites and your library career

Abstract: This chapter provides an overview of social networking and social media; it highlights the phenomenal growth in the usage of social networks and provides evidence that these growing networks are changing the face of online communication. The chapter emphasises the need for LIS professionals to participate in social networking while being aware of some of the issues. The chapter identifies three social networking sites: Facebook, LinkedIn and Twitter, and provides some first steps for LIS professionals to get started on exploring the career uses of these sites.

Key words: career, Web 2.0, LIS professionals, librarians, social networking sites, LinkedIn, Facebook, Twitter.

Social networking overview

If you work in libraries and information services and are not already using some of the social networks, you are probably slipping behind your net-savvy colleagues and the Internet active public–at–large. In the latter years of the past decade, social media sites such as Twitter have gone from hosting the fringe activities of geeks to being part of mainstream social media activity. Despite the media attention given to social networking, you may still wonder what all the fuss is about, and what role, if any, Facebook, LinkedIn, or Twitter can play in your career development.

In this chapter I provide background information about the growth in social networking and put this into a career context. I also explain the terminology and provide some compelling reasons why librarians need to take note of this important and dynamic growth area of communication technology. Finally, I look at the threats and opportunities of online social networking and provide you with tips on what to do and what not to do when you begin. By doing so you can still join the social media revolution and avoid some of the pitfalls these networks may pose in your career journey. This chapter will enable you to take some basic small steps, while you are considering your long-term strategy.

The impulse to communicate, to connect and form groups is as old as humanity. The promise of the Internet from the start was to bring about greater connectivity between people and groups in an online environment. Web 2.0 has accelerated this connectivity. Many library users, particularly those who are Millennials (those born between 1980–95), are leading the way in establishing personal profiles on social networking sites, and contributing information in the Web 2.0 environment. Whether you work in a public library, special school, academic library or information service, you will have discovered that many of your clients are totally comfortable in the online social environment. Those of us who work in colleges and universities know that today's students spend vast amounts of time on sites such as Facebook and MySpace, while libraries grapple with how to cater for this form of literacy. Let us first look at social networking software and how it works, so we can fully understand how these technologies can help us professionally.

What is social networking software?

Social networking software was developed to enhance human interaction on the web and to enable users to contribute to and adapt web content, by changing existing content or writing new content. Some examples of this are blogs, where users write content and wikis, where users change content. Social networking puts the control with us: we become the authors. These technologies have enormous appeal as they are built around our human need to communicate. The software itself presents few barriers to the end user; it is easy to understand and easy to access. And since most social networking products are free to use at the basic entry level, their uptake has been rapid around the online world.

It is worth pausing, to look at a few social network/social media definitions that are in common use. However, as with Web 2.0, there is no common agreement on definitions. How you define social networking will probably depend on whether you work in marketing, education, information technology or elsewhere.

The Wikipedia definition of a *social network service* is that:

> A *social network service* focuses on building and reflecting on social networks or social relations among people, for example, who share interests and/or activities. A social network service essentially consists of a representation of each user (often a profile), his/her social links, and a variety of additional services. (Wikipedia, Social networking sites)

American educator Ulises Mejias provides another definition of social networking software that comes close to the meaning LIS professionals could relate to since it incorporates the idea of networking and leveraging our networks, an idea that is relevant to careers. Mejias refers to social networking software as: 'software that allows people to interact and collaborate online or that aggregates the actions of networked users' (2005).

Now we will look at some of the different types of social networking sites. Broadly speaking there are two types: those that are centred around an individual's *profile* and shared interests, such as Facebook and LinkedIn, and those centred around an individual's shared *activities,* such as Flickr for photo sharing, YouTube for video sharing and SlideShare for sharing presentation slides. Throughout the book I will be expounding ideas for using these different types of social networking sites to advance your career.

What is social media?

Related to social networking software is the term 'social media', which tends to be used by those working in publishing and broadcasting. In other words 'social media' has a more media-specific meaning.

Wikipedia defines *social media* in this way:

> *Social media* are media for social interaction, using highly accessible and scalable publishing techniques. Social media use web-based technologies to transform and broadcast media monologues into social media dialogues. (Wikipedia, Social media)

Examples of social media are blogging, microblogging and social networking generally. The terms social networking and social media are sometimes used interchangeably. I will use both terms throughout the book. Whatever term is used, the overall picture is one of unprecedented global growth in social networking and social media.

The rise and rise of social networking

In March 2010, Heather Dougherty, Director of Research at the Internet market research company Hitwise, cited statistics showing that for the first time during the week of 13–19 March 2010, visits to the Facebook social networking site had surpassed Google site visits in the United States (Dougherty, 2010 and Figure 2.1 below). This was an important milestone, which clearly shows the relentless growth in social networking. Also, in that week the visits to Facebook had increased 185 per cent compared to the same

Figure 2.1   **Facebook growth from Hitwise**

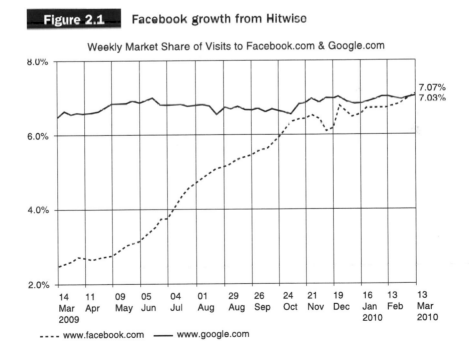

week in March 2009; visits to Google had increased by just 9 per cent during the same time frame. So while Google was still growing, Facebook far outstripped that growth in this twelve month period.

The Hitwise market research data is based on 10 million US Internet users accessing more than 1 million websites, across more than 160 industries in the United States.

This phenomenal social networking growth is being experienced worldwide. The Nielsen Company statistics show similar patterns, with some nations ahead of the United States in terms of time spent networking online. (See Table 2.1.)

The global reach of social networking and the time spent online per week, per person is substantial. The Nielsen statistics reflect only the activity in ten industrialised nations. We know that social networking is growing in popularity in

Table 2.1 The Nielsen Company statistics of global social networking usage

Social networking usage by country home and work/Feb 2010	
Country	Time per person per week hours: mins: secs
Average	5:27:33
Italy	6:27:53
Australia	6:25:21
United States	6:02:34
United Kingdom	5:50:56
Spain	4:50:49
Brazil	4:27:54
France	4:12:01
Germany	3:47:24
Switzerland	3:26:06
Japan	2:37:07

China, with some figures indicating that 92 per cent of 'netizens' (those actively involved in online communities) in China use social media. In China, the social network Qzone (from Tencent Inc.) is increasing at a similar rate to Facebook.

Nielsen statistics show a spread of users across the major sites, with Facebook predominating (see Table 2.2).

| Table 2.2 | The Nielsen Company statistics of social network traffic February 2010 |

	Global social network traffic February 2010		
Website	Per cent reach of active social users	Sessions per person	Time per person hours: mins: secs
Facebook	52	19.16	5:52:00
Myspace.com	15	6.66	0:59:33
Twitter.com	10	5.81	0:36:43
LinkedIn	6	3.15	0:12:47
Classmates Online	5	3.20	0:13:55

How long can this astonishing growth in social networking be sustained? Will the bubble burst at some stage? We can but speculate. However, if and when these companies disappear, or merge, they will surely be replaced by others with a similar goal: to engage in the commerce of connecting people online. Given the key drivers of growth which I outline below, I cannot foresee any slowing down for some years yet.

Drivers of social networking growth

The first thing to notice is that the software is appealing to more Internet users in the industrialised world; second, the devices used to access the software are proliferating; third, there are more access options. Anyone with a smart phone and an available connection can connect to Twitter, Facebook and other sites.

The range of network access options is another factor in growth. Wired access is just one method for people to connect to the Internet generally and to online social networks. Another method is via public or private wireless network or via mobile phone networks. In developing countries mobile access is often more readily available than wired access. So that is another growth factor. The ubiquity of wireless access and smart phones will continue to boost social networking usage.

What is so revolutionary about social networking software?

The pervasiveness of these social networks, and the range of devices for connecting, has led social media gurus to call the changes revolutionary (Carruthers, 2010). By comparison, the early 1990s now seems like the dark ages of the Internet. Then, access was available solely within academic, scientific and research networks and librarians and information technology professionals were the gatekeepers who mediated public network access. Obviously, this is no longer the case. Now social networking and social media are part of the mainstream.

Social networking usage demographics are changing too. Although usage of social networking sites, particularly MySpace, initially started among the so-called 'digital natives' or Millennials, the user demographic has shifted. By 2010, Facebook's fastest growing user segment was no longer college students, but women in the 55 to 65 age range. We can expect that demographics will continue to shift and change as new network options and methods of access appear.

In the very near future all new mobile phones will be smart phones and have inbuilt Internet capability. The Apple iPad, iPhone, Android and Blackberry are all devices that are Internet-enabled. Ebook readers with net capabilities add more new devices into the mix. Many of these come with the built-in social networking applications that make these devices so popular. Then, so long as we can pay for connectivity, we can connect whenever we like, wherever there is wireless and/or mobile phone coverage. Connectivity may be in the street, in a café, on the bus, at work, or at home. There is widespread availability of free Internet and wireless in many countries within public precincts, libraries, commercial facilities and elsewhere. With embedded geo location (real-world geographic location) available on new mobile digital devices, our movements may be pinpointed, which has implications for privacy and security that need to be considered.

What is exciting in social networking growth, when looked at from the global perspective, is the potential for mobile technologies to enable some developing countries to leapfrog the wired connection stage and jump into mobile connectivity. This may help to bridge the digital divide. Currently in the developing world hard-wired cable, fibre and copper wire connections may be unreliable, or unavailable. But in urban areas there can be mobile phone coverage. For example, in some African countries, such as Botswana and Namibia, mobile phone usage is comparatively high (Kujawski, 2009).

All this amounts to a *revolution* – a global, social network of ideas, information, conversations and friendships. However, we need to examine what this really means for us as library and information professionals.

Why should librarians be interested in social networking?

Previously, the only professional networks worth considering for our career development were the informal networks of colleagues and the formal networks, such as the professional library associations and societies. Today, additionally, we have many commercial social networks. Admittedly, these have been set up as business enterprises, but they can be harnessed to supplement the traditional methods of networking. With half a billion people on Facebook alone (and the figures keep climbing), social media sites have become a goldmine for their developers. But why should librarians be interested in this phenomenon? Should we not be wary of their obvious commercial imperative? Besides, are not most of the online conversations on Facebook or Twitter social, rather than professional, in nature? And who has time for these time wasting diversions? These are some of the objections to social networking that come up regularly. I will address these objections initially below. Furthermore, throughout the book I will provide career reasons for incorporating these and other networks into professional practice.

The OCLC report *Sharing, Privacy and Trust in Our Networked World* (2007) found that US library managers were less likely than the general public to use social networking sites. On the other hand, library managers were seen as digitally literate pioneers, having been online for a larger span of years than the general public at the time the survey was conducted. The same report found that for librarians in the 22 to 49 age range usage of social networking sites was level with the general public. This indicates some age differences among US librarians in their willingness to engage in social networking, although this would have changed since 2007. The point is that LIS professionals need to embrace social media or risk becoming irrelevant in an increasingly connected world. Australian social media expert and educationalist, Kate Carruthers, states: 'the willingness and desire to be hyperconnected via technology will become the new generation gap' (2010).

Indeed, social media cannot be ignored by anyone working in a public service area, from educators to librarians. Educators are seeing the Web 2.0 phenomenon as providing enormous potential to deliver services and engage students in the online environment. In Chapters 6 and 7, I will explore the potential of Web 2.0 for our own lifelong learning and professional development. As outlined in Chapter 1, Web 2.0, and by implication social networking, is totally aligned with the core business of libraries. Its use is therefore critical to the careers of LIS workers, both for performing our professional roles, and for personal development.

In my experience there is still some reluctance on the part of many LIS professionals to put themselves out there in the online world, as privacy is still a key concern. In our profession, we guard our privacy and tend not to be very good at self-promotion. The professional ethos supports guarding the privacy of library users too. But you need to actively use the Web 2.0 social media to fully understand their potential. If you are concerned about your privacy, you should pay particular attention to the advice given in Chapter 5. In that chapter I argue that you can engage online and maintain some of your privacy. This will always be a balancing act between participation and privacy. Each individual needs to work through the issues and decide for themselves.

What are the main issues or problems with social networking?

Whereas joining a social networking site may seem like an innocuous activity to some, as professionals we need to think hard about the implications of putting ourselves online. The first question to ask is: is it necessary to start networking socially? My answer is yes; as I have stated above, I think it is important to join in the conversation. And if you are reading this book you already have some interest in the topic. I will endeavour to convince you that it is worth it for your own career.

When using any of the social networks one of the important issues to keep in mind is *context*. Ask yourself why you are using the particular network. The common mistake users of social networking sites make is to not align their activities on the site with the purpose for which the network was set up. So firstly, ascertain what the parameters of the network are; and secondly, decide how you wish to use the network to advance your career. Then, aim to keep your interactions within these parameters. Each social networking site is different, with some more aligned to professional networking than others. For example, LinkedIn is first and foremost a professional network, so you should keep all your interactions on this network professional in nature. On the other hand, Facebook and MySpace are networks that provide a more personal, friendly, family context. However, this is changing now that Facebook provides the facility for group pages, which may be linked to a group or business.

One impact of Web 2.0 is that it is constantly pushing the boundaries. In our desire to participate we may just go with the flow without thinking of how particular softwares may sit with career goals. In terms of keeping to the context,

I find it unhelpful, for example, to have all my Twitter feed going into my LinkedIn profile. I choose some to go into LinkedIn and some not because I use these two social networks for quite different purposes. I do not necessarily want my professional connections to receive my social 'tweets', such as where the best coffee can be had in my neighbourhood. In older style online forums and discussion boards, some of this type of online communication may have been described as OT or 'off-topic' and would therefore have been discouraged or kept to a minimum. In other words, the users or members of the forum were drifting outside the purpose for which the site was set up. Web 2.0 challenges us and moves us outside such strictures. However, as professionals operating in the open social networking environment, we must keep the audience in the back of our minds. That audience may be just friends and colleagues, or it may include employers. Remember that information put online could be there forever.

In this chapter we have looked at the phenomenal growth in social media. In future chapters we will be looking at particular applications, such as for marketing, professional networking and professional development. I now briefly introduce three social networks: LinkedIn, Facebook and Twitter.

LinkedIn

LinkedIn is a business-oriented social networking site that has been around since 2003. It is an invaluable network for professionals wishing to establish an online profile and broaden their networks. Many employers are now using LinkedIn to find suitable applicants for positions and as a member you would be able to search for jobs there.

The LinkedIn website describes the site in this way:

> LinkedIn is the world's largest professional network, with over 70 million members and growing rapidly. LinkedIn connects you to your trusted contacts and helps you exchange knowledge, ideas, and opportunities with a broader network of professionals. (*http://www .linkedin.com/nhome/*)

There is no particular LIS chapter or section on LinkedIn, but there are several LIS groups, which I will look at in Chapter 3.

Facebook

Facebook is the most mainstream of all the social media and probably needs no introduction. According to recent statistics, 80 per cent of employers now use Facebook to check out potential job candidates. But Facebook is as much an opportunity as a threat in job hunting. You can use it to show yourself in the best possible light. By entering your public details, such as information on your work experience, hobbies, interests and qualifications, you can give people (including employers) a positive impression. Some observers of social media say that Facebook is about who you already know, whereas Twitter is about who you want to get to know.

Twitter

Of the entire current crop of social networks mentioned above, Twitter pushes the boundaries more than any other. The Twitter microblogging tool is a game changer in the sense that it is now being used in ways that were not envisioned by its creators. The purpose of Twitter is to provide a tool where individuals can post brief updates on what they are doing at a particular point in time. It is very hard to pin down in terms of when and where to use it professionally, since it crosses the context barriers I referred to above. The boundaries between the private and public life are blurred on Twitter. Many have dismissed it as a time waster. Steve Wheeler on his *Learning with 'e's* blog says, partly in jest, that there are those who get Twitter and those who do not. He finds it to be one of the most useful Web 2.0 tools for learning.

Wikipedia describes Twitter in this way:

> Twitter is a social networking and microblogging service that enables its users to send and read other user messages called tweets. Tweets are text-based posts of up to 140 characters displayed on the author's profile page. Tweets are publicly visible by default; however senders can restrict message delivery to their friends' list. Users may subscribe to other author tweets — this is known as following and subscribers are known as followers ... all users can send and receive tweets via the Twitter website, compatible external applications (such as, for smart phones), or by Short Message Service (SMS) available in certain countries. While the service is free, accessing it through SMS may incur phone service provider fees. (Wikipedia, Twitter)

By late 2010 there were reportedly 175 million users of Twitter worldwide.

LinkedIn, Facebook and Twitter and their particular features and professional uses will be more fully explored in Chapter 3 and subsequent chapters. To conclude this chapter,

I provide you with some actions to get you started on your social network journey.

Getting started on the social networking checklist

- *Look at three social networking sites:*
  Using the URLs provided in this chapter's reference list, take a look at LinkedIn, Facebook and Twitter. Be aware of context and decide which of these sites fits a professional purpose for you. Think strategically and decide which sites will benefit you.

- *Look at each network's profile options:*
  Each of the three sites will require you to add a profile, or brief description of yourself. Ask yourself what professional image you want to project on this particular network. Think about choosing a unique user name that can be used for all your social network profiles. I will be saying a lot more about developing profiles in Chapters 3 and 4. For now, you need to be aware that eventually your profile will become the entry point where future employers can find you.

- *Connections:*
  Seek out some of your face-to-face colleagues who use social networks and ask them to join you in the future as a 'friend' on your network. In this way, you can start to build a network of contacts. If you are a student or new graduate you could find suitable online connections among your colleagues, fellow students, tutors, lecturers, mentors or any fellow professionals.

- *Privacy:*
  Read through the network's privacy policy and terms of use. In the future you may need to review your privacy

settings and keep up with privacy changes. Chapters 3 and 5 will cover privacy in detail.

In the next chapter I will delve into the relative advantages of LinkedIn, Facebook or Twitter and will give instructions on how to use them professionally.

Conclusion

Social media use is growing exponentially. Some pundits see this as a new frontier of human connectedness. Social networking sites also help us to take charge of our careers, help us to work independently, and give us more control over who we network with. As such, they put power into our hands as librarians to be strategic in our networking. If we consider the Six Degrees of Separation principle (that everyone on the planet is at most six connections away from any other person), then it is remarkable who we can connect with now. I will look into the role of networking in careers in Chapter 8. In this chapter I have presented the benefits of a new set of online career tools. But the reality check is: do not throw the baby out with the bathwater; societies, organisations, conferences, seminars, in-service courses are still valid professional development activities. The new social tools will be a supplement to the tried and true, face-to-face professional methods of networking.

References

Carruthers, K. (2010) *Digital Revolution Not Going Away. Aide memoire* (blog). Retrieved 4 September 2010, from *http://katecarruthers.com/blog/2010/06/digital-revolution-not-going-away/*.

Dougherty, H. (2010) *Facebook Reached Top Ranking*. Retrieved 2 July 2010, from *http://weblogs.hitwise.com/heather-dougherty/2010/03/facebook_reaches_top_ranking_i.html*.

Kujawski, M. (2009) *Latest Mobile Phone Statistics from Africa and What This Means*. Retrieved 1 July 2010, from *http://www.mikekujawski.ca/2009/03/16/latest-mobile-phone-statistics-from-africa-and-what-this-means/*.

Mejias, U. (2005) *A Nomad's Guide to Learning and Social Software*. Retrieved 1 July, 2010, from *http://knowledge tree.flexiblelearning.net.au/edition07/download/la_mejias .pdf*.

OCLC (2007) *Sharing, Privacy and Trust in our Networked World*: A Report to the OCLC membership. Dublin, OH: OCLC Online Computer Library Center, Inc.

Useful weblinks

Mashable/Social Media (blog). Global social media usage. *http://mashable.com/2010/03/19/global-social-media-usage* Hitwise. *http://www.hitwise.com/us*

Facebook. Statistical data at 30 May 2010. *http://www .facebook.com/press/info.php?statistics*

Facebook Home: *http://www.facebook.com/login.php*

LinkedIn Home: *http://www.linkedin.com/nhome/*

The Nielsen Company: *http://blog.nielsen.com/*

Twitter Home: *http://twitter.com/*

Wheeler, Steve. Learning with 'e's (blog). *http://steve-wheeler .blogspot.com/*

Wikipedia. Social media: *http://en.wikipedia.org/wiki/Social_ media*

Wikipedia. Social networking sites. *http://en.wikipedia.org/ wiki/Social_networking_sites*

Wikipedia. Twitter: *http://en.wikipedia.org/wiki/Twitter*

3

Using Facebook, LinkedIn and Twitter for your career

Abstract: This chapter focuses on three social networking sites: Facebook, LinkedIn and Twitter, providing an overview of the features of each site. It describes how you can set up a professional profile on each site to support your library career; and it identifies the key features that differentiate each site and provides some context to enable professionals to choose the best site(s) for their particular career purpose(s). The chapter also provides a list of tips and some dos and don'ts for Facebook, LinkedIn and Twitter so that you can use them more effectively.

Key words: career, Web 2.0, LIS professionals, librarians, social networking sites, LinkedIn, Facebook, Twitter.

In this chapter I continue on from the social networking theme in Chapter 2 and expand on three major social networking sites: Facebook, LinkedIn and Twitter. I describe their strengths and particular features, and why they could be incorporated into your career thinking. And I explain how each has its own particular use for professional ventures. However, this will not be an exhaustive account; reference will be made in future chapters to the three sites, as they have applications in marketing, networking, mentoring and professional development.

Facebook

You have probably read in the press about employees being sacked or disgraced after their employer found a revealing photo or some other incriminating evidence about the employee on Facebook. Some employers are now strategically screening prospective job candidates by searching them out on Facebook, so you need to be wary of this, while appreciating how it can be used to your advantage.

I spoke in Chapter 2 about the rapid growth of Facebook, which is astounding, considering the network has been around for just six years. It may be useful to reflect on where this global Facebook network came from, and who is behind it. Facebook was started in 2004, by the then Harvard student Mark Zuckerberg. It was initially called 'thefacebook.com', and the intention was to emulate the printed student yearbooks, that were called 'facebooks', which included the names and photographs of every Harvard undergraduate. From Harvard, the network spread to other Ivy League universities, and in 2006 Facebook was extended to anyone with e-mail. Developers were invited to contribute in 2007 and they started writing applications for Facebook, providing such things as games, gift giving, and photo sharing. With the proliferation of new Facebook applications the network evolved to become what it is today.

Here are some impressive Facebook facts as of mid-2010:

- Facebook is the world's largest social network;
- it has over 400 million members, and membership is rising by 5 per cent a month;
- 20 per cent of people on the Internet are on Facebook;
- 'Facebook' is the most searched term on search engines;
- 50 per cent of members log in each day, spending on average one hour per day;

- three-quarters of members are outside the United States;
- 25 per cent of members access the network via a mobile device;
- the average member has 130 friends.

Facebook is like an internet within the Internet: it is a closed network of 'friends' that has all the characteristics of a casual, online meeting place. Non-members need to join the network if they wish, for example, to view a Facebook member's photos. But few of us consider the power the network wields and the commercial imperative driving it, although some of the news reports about identity threats, misuse of personal data and stalking have sounded warning bells. Despite the bad press, many libraries and librarians are actively using this social network, so we need to understand how it works.

Librarian awareness of Facebook

When Charnigo and Barnett-Ellis (2007) surveyed librarians, many of the respondents were not aware of the possibility that, in addition to being a social site, Facebook could be both a professional meeting place and a potential source of networking. For example, many professionals are now using this social networking site to establish connections with old friends and colleagues, and most professional library organisations, publishers and library suppliers have a presence on Facebook. As the following section shows, Facebook is more than just a communication mechanism.

Library activity on Facebook

Facebook provides additional functionality that enables you to set up 'groups' and 'pages'. Facebook groups and Facebook pages are similar to websites and provide an online environment where you can add contact information, events, promotions, news, photos and videos. However, you need to be a member of Facebook to join a group or access a Facebook page. This is one way Facebook attracts new members. Some examples of library and librarian activity on Facebook are:

- professional associations and interest group pages;
- library groups and pages;
- publishers' and library suppliers' groups and pages;
- catalogue and database search applications, for example JSTOR, WorldCat and Pubmed;
- online chat within Facebook (could be used for library e-reference).

Through the many Facebook applications, a library's presence can be integrated with other Web 2.0 applications, thus extending and amplifying its Facebook presence. New features are being added to Facebook all the time to facilitate cross-linking with other social networking sites. For example, Facebook now uses social plug-ins that appear on other web-sites and social networking sites. For this feature Facebook uses the 'thumbs-up' symbol, so you can register your interest in something on another site and then it will appear as a status update in your Facebook newsfeed, visible to all your Facebook friends. All of this increased linking boosts Facebook usage and makes its online activity more visible. This applies equally to the profile your library has and also your individual profile, which I will look at now.

How can librarians use Facebook?

You have seen how social networking sites offer enormous potential for fostering community and sharing of interests.

Now I want you to realise that by using Facebook you can perform a range of professional activities, such as:

- setting up and joining professional groups;
- collaborating with colleagues who are on Facebook;
- chatting with online colleagues in real time;
- sharing event photos, videos, blog posts and news;
- linking other Web 2.0 applications into your Facebook.

But does this come at a price in terms of our privacy?

Facebook and privacy

Privacy has been a major concern for Facebook users ever since the network's beginning in 2004. Facebook does have privacy settings; however, many Facebook users are unaware of the standard default settings and that they can change these settings when they join the network. This is not surprising because over the past few years there have been numerous changes to privacy settings, and the average user does not keep abreast of these changes. As a consequence, users do not lock down their personal information.

One breach-of-privacy allegation against Facebook is that the company uses members' private information. For example, unprivatised personal photos may be used for other purposes, such as to advertise merchandise to members' Facebook friends.

Facebook founder, Mark Zuckerberg, is on the record as saying (in effect) that the age of privacy is dead and that privacy social norms were evolving (Kirkpatrick 2010). There is some truth in this: the Web 2.0 era of openness and sharing is pushing the envelope on privacy, and public attitudes are changing – especially in younger generations; however, a significant number of people guard their privacy jealously (Chapter 5 on privacy will explore this important topic in more detail).

Because of lack of privacy and other Orwellian issues to do with the power of the Facebook network, such as the difficulty of deleting accounts, there has been a backlash against Facebook. On 31 May 2010 a cohort of users declared official 'quit Facebook day' and went to great lengths to delete their accounts and withdraw from the network. However, Facebook statistics show that more users joined than left the network on that day, so the overall effect of the backlash was minimal. However, the 'quit Facebook day' movement refocused people's attention on the network's image and privacy issues.

Privacy is just one of many tensions in Web 2.0, reflecting our desire to participate and share in the openness of the online environment, and our counteracting fear that this is a risky undertaking.

Facebook and employers

As mentioned above, Facebook was not established as a professional network. The reason most people join it is for the social and entertainment aspects: communicating with family and friends, uploading photos, sharing links and videos, playing online games. So what is its advantage for career development? We have seen above that library groups and associations are using Facebook and shaping it to their needs. There are potential implications for job seekers too.

Potential employers may be able to find you on Facebook. At this stage, Facebook profiles are not retrieved via Google or other search engines. Therefore, employers would need to be a Facebook member and use the Facebook member search facility to find you on Facebook. In this way, you could be found, although given the size of the network now, the potential for mistaken identity is real. Therefore, if you wish your professional image to be found, you need to professionalise your Facebook profile.

Even if you are not currently looking for employment, you should aim to build a positive, professional looking profile on Facebook. And no matter how savvy you are, you should not assume that your activities on Facebook will be private, so it is best to follow the guidelines below on how to set up your LIS professional Facebook profile. If you are totally new to Facebook their help pages guide you through the process of registering, entering your e-mail, name and password and finding friends. The relevant pages are:

- Facebook Help Center: *http://www.facebook.com/help/*

- Facebook Getting Started: *http://www.facebook.com/help/?guide*

- Facebook Profile set-up: *http://www.facebook.com/help/?guide=set_up_profile*

Facebook tips

Remember that your profile is your 'landing page' on Facebook, where even those who are not your existing 'friends' may find you. If someone searches for your name within Facebook, this is where they will land. Make sure you put a professional looking photo of yourself there, as nothing looks worse than a blank profile image on Facebook. How much the public and those not on your friends list can see of your profile will depend on how you restrict your privacy. For example, you could try to restrict access to your photos. However, as we have seen above, these privacy adjustments are tricky to master and Facebook keeps changing the rules. It is probably safer to assume that all of your profile is available and plan accordingly.

Here are some ideas on creating a professional looking Facebook profile:

- set up a profile that is authentic, includes your interests, hobbies and qualifications and a professional looking profile photo;
- think about your audience, assume that an employer may find you on Facebook and put yourself in their shoes;
- assume that all your information and photos are publicly accessible;
- add links to your professional development activities, and your other sites (your blog or website);
- control your privacy settings and do not assume the default privacy settings are sufficient;
- take ownership and responsibility of your profile and keep it up to date.

To sum up: there are professional uses for Facebook. It has merit as a site to showcase a positive work-related profile and as a place for making professional LIS contacts. However, you need to be mindful that Facebook's *raison d'être* is as a casual and non-professional meeting place. Arguably, a far better professional network is the much smaller business and professional networking site, LinkedIn.

LinkedIn

LinkedIn has been likened to a business version of Facebook. It is an online network for professionals showcasing their work-related capabilities and connections. Like Facebook, it is a network centred on your individual profile, which can be accessed by other members of the site. A limited LinkedIn profile can also be made available as a public search, which can be retrieved by search engines, such as Google. LinkedIn lacks the frivolity and fun aspect of Facebook, as it is a purpose-built professional online network. The other characteristic of LinkedIn worth noting is that because it is indexed on Google, a well constructed LinkedIn profile can reach out to a global network of LIS professionals. You are much more discoverable on LinkedIn than on Facebook and many employers now use LinkedIn to find suitable persons to fill positions. But quite apart from its usefulness for job seeking, LinkedIn is a valuable site for networking with colleagues within and without the LIS area.

LinkedIn was established in 2003, with the network headquarters located in California. Although smaller than Facebook, it is growing in size and influence in the business world. By 2004 it had reached 1 million members; then, by October 2009, according to the LinkedIn blog, the network had 50 million users worldwide and was growing at the rate of about one new member per second.

Some impressive LinkedIn facts as of mid-2010 (source LinkedIn blog):

- LinkedIn has over 70 million members;
- network members are found in over 200 countries;
- LinkedIn has about 4 million members in the UK;
- LinkedIn has around 1 million members in Australia;
- 80 per cent of companies in the United States use LinkedIn to find staff;
- all Fortune 500 company executives are LinkedIn members.

There are several levels of LinkedIn accounts:

- the free, basic LinkedIn account, which is adequate for an individual professional;

■ three levels of premium business LinkedIn accounts, which have additional features such as greater tools for networking, finding contacts and communicating.

Businesses are now creating profiles and placing jobs on LinkedIn, which means you can find out more about a particular organisation and check them out. Furthermore, job opportunities will be suggested to you by the system, depending on what keywords you have included in your profile. I will discuss some ways to maximise your profile below.

LinkedIn uses the tag line *Relationships Matter,* which is apt because it is a most useful network for visibly marketing the work of professionals, helping them to make contacts and build relationships. Like other social networking sites, LinkedIn gives you the power to connect with your friends and with your friends' friends. This lays out a web of connections to people who may be personal friends, colleagues, or potential employers. If you work to develop your network, LinkedIn offers a myriad of possibilities. My recommendation would be to make LinkedIn one of the key Web 2.0 tools in your career development kit.

When would you get started on using this network? Many students are now starting out with building a LinkedIn presence while still completing their courses, so it is never too early. If you are new to LinkedIn, start by setting up a profile and, as with Facebook, this is the landing page where other LinkedIn members will find you. There is a public version of your profile which you can opt to make available. Do this, as this is the public profile that will be found via Google, as mentioned above. Newcomers to LinkedIn should look through the videos and help pages on the website. The relevant pages that will help you to get started are:

- LinkedIn Learning Center: *http://learn.linkedin.com/*
- LinkedIn Profile Help: *http://learn.linkedin.com/profiles/ overview/*
- LinkedIn Blog: *http://blog.linkedin.com/*

LinkedIn headline and summary paragraph

Start setting up your profile by writing a headline, which includes your current position and the name of your current employer. Then write a good summary paragraph about yourself. The summary paragraph should emphasise what you are doing now in your current job and what you can do. It is here you put your best foot forward, so include information here that will interest prospective employers, such as any projects you are working on, and your key capabilities. Remember that you can update and change your profile summary to reflect new directions or new emphases. When writing your summary, add some pertinent keywords relating to your work interests, as this will help employers to find you via the LinkedIn search. There is an example of a LinkedIn profile in Figure 3.1.

LinkedIn adding connections

The LinkedIn site suggests that you accept connections only to people you know personally. However, you are not obliged to follow this advice because some social networking gurus disagree with LinkedIn's recommendation on this point. Who to add as connections will depend on where you are in your career journey. LIS students or early-career professionals may wish to add fellow or former student colleagues,

Figure 3.1 LinkedIn profile

other early-career colleagues, tutors or lecturers or library managers. Established LIS professionals may wish to branch out more widely to add professional contacts outside their immediate work area and outside the profession at large. Start with a few and then check to see who these people have connections with. The power of social networking is to build up a network based on your contacts' contacts, as I have discussed.

Seeking recommendations on LinkedIn

Get some strong recommendations from your manager, or professional contacts to round out your profile. Ask them to identify your strengths and abilities.

Add links and Web 2.0 applications

Add a link into your profile to any of your other Web 2.0 applications, such as your website, if you have one. Also add RSS feeds from your blog and your SlideShare presentations (I will be covering RSS and SlideShare in future chapters). There are some purpose-built LinkedIn applications that help you do this. Look for 'Applications' and 'Blog link' on the profile page. You can also link in your Twitter feed, if you have a professional related Twitter account; I recommend that you maintain the professional context of LinkedIn and *not add all* the Twitter feed, which can detract from LinkedIn's professionalism. However, with the Twitter LinkedIn integration you can feed *some* of your Twitter tweets into LinkedIn by setting up this integration and giving your tweets the hash tag #in. There is more about Twitter hash tags below. Twitter is often used more as a casual network, and blurs contexts, as I will discuss below.

Join some LinkedIn LIS groups

There are quite a number of librarian groups on LinkedIn, so it makes good career sense to join one or two of these groups and start contributing to the conversations. To find LinkedIn library groups, you need to do a search for library or librarians under the Groups function. Some library groups I have come across are:

■ LinkedIn American Library Association (ALA) Group page;

■ LinkedIn LIS Career Options Group page (subgroup of LinkedIn ALA);

■ LinkedIn CILIP: the Chartered Institute of Library and Information Professionals Group page.

LinkedIn tips

The above pointers will get you started on exploiting the professional potential of LinkedIn. Some further words of advice for rounding out your LinkedIn profile are to:

- Write your LinkedIn profile keeping a present or future employer firmly in mind.
- Add a professional looking profile photo.
- Include your education, capabilities, experience and qualifications.
- Include your professional associations, affiliations, and any awards.
- Add links to your blog or website, if you have one.
- Adjust your privacy settings and plan to keep most of your LinkedIn profile public.
- Take responsibility for your profile, keep it up to date and check regularly for new features in LinkedIn.
- Think long term and start early to build your network of contacts.

There are some excellent books, guides and blog posts on how to use LinkedIn for business and professional purposes. For example, Guy Kawasaki (2007) has some tips on ways to use your LinkedIn profile. I have listed some of these books and web links in the reference list at the end of this chapter. I will return to LinkedIn in future chapters. It is an important Web 2.0 social network to help with two cornerstones of LIS career development: networking and marketing.

Twitter

Twitter is a popular social networking site for microblogging. The premise behind Twitter is that network members post brief messages in response to the hypothetical question: 'What's happening?' Twitter has been called the SMS of the Internet because its 140-character post limitation matches the limitation of an SMS or text message.

As a social networking site, Twitter operates quite differently from Facebook and LinkedIn. With Twitter you first set up a profile and then start to build some connections among fellow members. The brief postings you send via Twitter are known as 'tweets'. All your tweets are visible to the public network unless you change the default settings to restrict access. However, the majority of users keep their tweets on open access. You can subscribe to other members' tweets and 'follow' them. Twitter can be accessed from an online wired, networked computer or from a mobile device.

If you feel that the whole idea behind Twitter sounds rather frivolous or pointless, you are not alone. It is probably the most misunderstood social network, and this misunderstanding is probably what divides people into those who 'get it' and those who do not. I admit to having been a Twitter sceptic at one stage, but now I find it to be an incredibly simple, yet powerful tool for communication, networking and information sharing. However, it is certainly not the case that once you try Twitter you will become a devotee. Many new users abandon Twitter because they are not willing or patient enough to build a critical mass of contacts. I estimate you need to follow about 50 to 100 people to fully exploit Twitter.

As with other social networking software, Twitter's growth has been outstanding in recent years. Twitter has a speed and immediacy unmatched by other social networks and it can emulate the quick flow of IM (Instant Messenger) when several parties are online and communicating at the same time.

Here are some Twitter stats in mid-2010:

- growth in the year 2009–10 was 1,400 per cent;
- 5,000 tweets per day in 2007;
- 300,000 tweets per day in 2008;
- 35 million tweets per day by the end of 2009;
- 50 million tweets per day by mid-2010 – an average of 600 tweets per second, with 10–15 million active users.

How does Twitter work?

If you want to give Twitter a try, start by going to the main website: *www.twitter.com* and establishing a free account. To do this you need to provide your name, e-mail address, a unique user name and then read the terms of agreement and privacy statement. It is helpful for your online identity to choose a username the same as, or similar to your other Web 2.0 social networks. However, sometimes you will find your name has already been taken, so have a back-up option. Add a brief statement about yourself, giving your areas of interest and including a link to your blog, website or any other online profile you may have. This is important in establishing your credentials on Twitter so that potential followers can check you out. If they like what they see they may decide to follow you. Include a professional-looking photo or avatar image. Then you are ready to start sending out some tweets.

Look around among your first few contacts for people to follow. Knowing who to follow is difficult at first, so finding a Twitter mentor may be helpful. Many bloggers place their Twitter feeds on their blogs, so that is a good way to find and follow experts in the field. The more contacts you add, the more the momentum picks up and the full potential of Twitter is revealed. It is quite acceptable to lurk for a while and listen in to conversations until you get the hang of

Twitter. But remember: it is a two-way conversation and *your* contribution is important.

Phil Bradley (2009) and Sue Waters (2010) each offer some useful Twitter getting-started hints for librarians and educators. (See the links at the end of this chapter.)

Twitter terminology

Having knowledge of the Twitter terminology will help you communicate more confidently when you start out. The terminology includes terms, abbreviations and conventions, such as:

- following – someone you are following (i.e. subscribing to their Twitter feed);
- followers – those who are following you (subscribing to your Twitter feed);
- @ – the code that identifies the individual Twitter member's name;
- RT – retweet another's tweet (retweet is done if you support another's tweet, some users clarify that this is not an endorsement);
- DM – a direct private message to a follower, like a short, private 140 character e-mail;
- # – a hash tag or type of keyword to identify the topic of your tweet, which can be searched;
- trending – the current hot topics on Twitter.

Most people use one of the Twitter clients (Twitter-specific programs) such as TweetDeck, HootSuite or Echofon, rather than the 'native interface' of the Twitter homepage. There are other Twitter clients for mobile devices such as Twitter for iPhone and Twitter for Blackberry. Twitter clients provide useful functionality that helps you organise your contacts into lists and keep track of Twitter activity during the day. See the screen of the Tweetdeck Twitter client in Figure 3.2.

Figure 3.2 Tweetdeck, the Twitter client

Twitter and privacy

According to the Harvard business blog, in 2009 more data was being generated by individuals than in the entire history of mankind up to 2008. However, whereas social networks, such as Facebook and Twitter, are free to join, there is a catch: the social media platform providers welcome us in because they can profit from our data. What we contribute on Facebook and Twitter is being data mined, so the less private we are the more data we make available to the data miners.

How does Twitter rate on the privacy issue? More than any other social networking site, Twitter blurs the lines between the private and the public self. We can choose to tweet privately to our friends and contacts alone, but few choose this option. All Twitter feeds are now being picked up by Google, Bing and Yahoo! Keep this in mind and think before you post a message. Colleagues or employers can read your tweets if they do a Google search for your name.

How might librarians use Twitter?

Twitter has applications for all areas of library career development: personal marketing networking, professional development and learning. Librarians around the world are already active users of Twitter. If you are willing to suspend your disbelief and give Twitter a try, you are likely to find it to be a very useful Web 2.0 tool. For example, LIS conferences are encouraging live tweeting and some presenters are incorporating a live Twitter stream into their presentations as a new way to engage with the conference audience. That way the offsite audience can also engage with conference activities.

In future chapters I will further explore the professional uses of Twitter and how it can amplify all of your Web 2.0 activity. Also I will also focus on privacy and Twitter in Chapter 5.

Twitter tips

I use Twitter as a professional learning and networking tool and some of my tips for the effective use of this site for your career are:

- choose your username, photo or avatar to reflect your professional image;
- add a brief biography to reflect your professional self;

- put a link on your Twitter profile to your blog or website, so that potential followers can check you out;

- start posting and look around for professional LIS people to follow;

- think before you post and assume all postings are being transmitted widely;

- be collegial and join in the conversations.

Finally, with all three networks, what you should consider is when to use them and how they fit in with your career goals. In future chapters I will address all these questions and suggest how the networks can be applied to your marketing, networking and professional development.

References

Bradley, P. (2009) *Twitter*. Retrieved 1 March, 2009, from *http://www.philb.com/twitter.htm*.

Charnigo, L. and Barnett-Ellis, P. (2007) Checking out Facebook.com: The Impact of a Digital Trend on Academic Libraries. *Information Technology and Libraries,* 26(1), 23.

Elad, J. (2009) *LinkedIn for Dummies*. Hoboken, NJ: John Wiley & Sons.

Kawasaki, G. (2007) *Ten Ways to Use LinkedIn*. Retrieved 2 September 2010, from *http://blog.guykawasaki.com/2007/01/ten_ways_to_use.html#axzz0tSSsFG9b*.

Kirkpatrick, D. (2010) *The Facebook Effect:The Inside Story of the Company that is Connecting the World*. New York: Simon & Schuster.

Kirkpatrick, M. (2010). Facebook's Zuckerberg says the age of privacy is over. Retrieved 23 August, 2011, from http://www.readwriteweb.com/archives/facebooks_zuckerberg_says_the_age_of_privacy_is_ov.php

Morris, T. (2010) *All a Twitter: a Personal and Professional Guide to Social Networking with Twitter*. Indianapolis, IN: Que.

Rutledge, P.A. (2010) *Using LinkedIn*. Indianapolis, IN.: Que.

Waters, S. (2010) *A Twitteraholics Guide to Tweets Hash Tags and All Things Twitter*. Retrieved 2 September 2010, from *http://theedublogger.com/2010/07/08/a-twitter aholics-guide-to-tweets-hashtags-and-all-things-twitter/*.

Useful weblinks

Carruthers, Kate. Digital revolution not going away: *http://katecarruthers.com/blog/2010/06/digital-revolution-not-going-away/*

Dority, Kim. LinkedIn: Everything I ever wanted to tell you, but was too shy/modest/embarrassed to say. *http://www.liscareer.com/dority_linkedin.htm*

Facebook home: *www.facebook.com*

Facebook and privacy: *http://techcrunch.com/2010/06/07/privacy-facebook-visitors/*

Harvard business blog: *http://blogs.harvardbusiness.org/now-new-next/2009/05/the-social-data-revolution.html*

Kawasaki, Guy. Facebook privacy: *http://techcrunch.com/2010/06/07/privacy-facebook-visitors/*

LinkedIn home: *http://www.linkedin.com/nhome/*

Twitter home: *http://twitter.com/*

Twitter and privacy: *http://twitter.com/privacy*

Twitter stats: *http://blog.twitter.com/2010/02/measuring-tweets.html*

4

Personal marketing
for your career

Abstract: This chapter focuses on marketing in LIS career development. It provides an overview of marketing principles (the four Ps and the four Cs) and applies these principles to personal brand building. The chapter also describes some self-analysis techniques that enable librarians and LIS professionals to reflect on their strengths and see themselves as a personal brand. Finally, the chapter identifies several Web 2.0 tools for brand development and provides a 'how to' action list for each tool.

Key words: career, Web 2.0, LIS professionals, librarians, social networking sites, marketing, personal marketing, personal brand, web presence, online identity, online profile, eportfolios, Twitter, LinkedIn, SlideShare.

If you have read the previous chapters, you will be aware that using the Web 2.0 social media tools gives you greater online visibility. Now you can start to build an online identity that helps your career. In this chapter I examine marketing and using particular Web 2.0 tools for personal marketing. Once you go online, you have a web presence or online identity of sorts. But this is likely to be fairly ad hoc. In this chapter you will learn how to take some control and have a planned web presence. You will also move further down the planned marketing route, taking advantage of the opportunities social media provide.

In my experience LIS professionals and librarians are not good at marketing, particularly self-marketing and promotion. There are reasons for this. The majority of LIS jobs are in the public sector, rather than the private sector, so marketing may not be practised as aggressively in the organisations we work for. If we do see ourselves as having a marketing role, we are more likely to act on behalf of our organisations by marketing our libraries or particular library services. Some of our resistance to personal marketing, particularly in the online environment, may relate to our views on privacy. As mentioned previously, the OCLC report, *Sharing, Privacy and Trust in Our Networked World*, found that librarians were less comfortable with revealing themselves online than the general public. Privacy is a crucial issue that will be examined in Chapter 5.

Several leaders in the LIS profession, such as Mary Ellen Bates (2003), Kim Dority (2006) and Scott Brown (2010), have begun to raise an awareness of the importance of marketing and developing a personal brand. Now that social networking is part of the marketing mix, the topic is very pertinent for all librarians.

What is marketing and why do you need to know about it?

Marketing is often confused with selling, or promotion, but these are just elements of the overall marketing picture. Marketing takes a broad view, looking at the approach to a product: where to position the product, how it is packaged and delivered, and how to communicate its value to the customer. The product could just as easily be a service (for example the library service), or a message, or an individual, which is what is meant when we talk about personal brand.

Marketing has been regarded as an important tool in LIS career development for some time. If you look around at the LIS career literature, most books have a chapter or two on marketing. In the career context, marketing is not just about job seeking, promoting yourself and differentiating yourself from the competition. It is also about taking a long-term approach to career development and thinking broadly about where your skills may take you, how to develop them, and how to work towards your career goals. If you are already in employment, it is about proving your worth and staying relevant to your clients and your library.

Many LIS professionals already market the library services and may even have a library marketing plan. The @ *your library* marketing campaign has been active in several countries over the past decade and has been successful in introducing many librarians to basic marketing concepts. I will now turn my attention to personal marketing and building a brand.

How do you apply marketing principles to your career?

The marketing mix refers to the *four ps,* the key elements of marketing: *product, promotion, place and price,* which need to be considered and worked through when marketing a product. The product can be an organisation, a service, or an individual person.

- *Product:* you are the product. Think about what makes you unique, what is your competitive advantage, where you would position yourself. Some of the brand self-assessment questions below will help you to develop your brand.
- *Promotion:* is about how you communicate the features and benefits of the product.

- *Place:* is about the distribution channel. In this case it could include your social network contacts and social networking tools (like LinkedIn).
- *Price:* would include your salary and work conditions and benefits you expect.

How do you start to develop a personal brand?

In the previous chapters I have given you some insights into how social networking can help you to develop your brand. For example, I gave advice on what to include in your online profile on LinkedIn and Twitter. However, it can be quite hard to get your head around the idea of seeing yourself as a brand. So, let us consider how this was done in the past, before online and social media were available to us. In the past, one of the cornerstones of LIS career plans was the printed résumé, curriculum vitae or career portfolio, where one listed one's achievements, gave an inventory of project work, volunteer work, or awards, and included skills and abilities. It was a fairly static written document that could be reviewed, updated and changed according to the current purpose. The résumé and CV included many of the elements that are needed to develop a brand. Now imagine all this in the online environment. Web 2.0 gives us a new set of tools to supplement, rather than replace, the old ways of doing things.

Personal brand self-assessment checklist

In order to start to develop your distinctive personal brand you need to think about yourself and your career, using the questions below. Respond to these questions in terms of a job you are applying for, a prospective project, or how you operate in the workplace:

- What is the image I wish to convey?
- What is distinctive about me?
- What benefits can I offer?
- What are my skills, capabilities and particular attributes?
- What are my strengths?
- Why would someone be interested in me?

SWOT analysis

Another useful tool for self assessment is the SWOT analysis technique, which involves identifying your key *strengths* and *weaknesses,* and the *opportunities* and *threats* in the external environment. In this analysis, focus first on the internal environment: look at yourself and analyse your strengths and weaknesses. If you are brave, you can ask colleagues to help you. Then focus on the external environment, which is the area you are working in, or planning to work in. What are the opportunities and threats in that environment? You may not be able to control this environment, but you still need to know and acknowledge the opportunities and threats inherent in it.

The elevator pitch

Yet another technique for developing a brand is the 'elevator pitch', which is to develop a brief verbal presentation, or sound grab, that will 'pitch' you to a potential employer. In fact, this technique can be used in many other workplace situations. It will include a summary of you and what you have to offer an employer. Or it may be a summary of you in your current job and what benefits you provide in the workplace. You are essentially selling yourself and your capabilities. Practise by synthesising what you do in your present job into a short, one-minute presentation. Use the ideas gained from the self-assessment above, or other cues from your profile on Twitter, or LinkedIn, covered in Chapter 3.

Developing a personal brand as an early-career professional

Students or early-career professionals, particularly those who are new to the LIS discipline, may be daunted at the prospect of thinking about themselves as a unique brand. But your studies will have given you some excellent material to work with, to help you create your brand. In fact, in some ways you are ahead of the game, as you should have the very latest professional information at your fingertips. My advice would be to focus on:

1. Your LIS studies: the subjects that appealed to you; your top assignment topics, and any project work or group work where you excelled.

2. Library practicums or internships: what you learned about yourself in the library workplace, and what kind of library work appealed to you.

3. Your general interests, especially those that relate to and support your profile.

4. The future: the sort of work you want to be doing that is the best fit for your skills.

5. Volunteer work or committee work you have done that enhanced or raised your profile.

Then, once you have fleshed out these topics and interests, offer to do a presentation, or write them up as a blog post.

Marketing: the four Cs

With the advent of Web 2.0 and social media marketing, you need to incorporate the four Cs into your marketing: *content, context, connections* and *conversations*. The meaning and some examples of these are:

- *content:* anything we contribute online such as blog posts, online slides, images or other media;
- *context:* where we share the content, for example on a blog, on LinkedIn, Facebook, Twitter;
- *connections:* the links with people in our networks;
- *conversations:* the interactions and conversations that can in turn help to create more content.

So, a whole range of our activities are entailed in creating our personal brand. The social media activities shown in Table 4.1 point the way to brand building using the marketing 4 Cs.

All of the above exercises would contribute to developing your authentic individual brand. The beauty of the current

Table 4.1 Personal brand building using the 4 Cs

Personal brand building checklist using the 4 Cs
■ Join a few social networking sites (**Connections**)
■ Develop a strong written summary or profile (**Content**)
■ Start to contribute content to a blog or other media (**Content**)
■ Integrate your relevant content across different networks (**Context**)
■ Connect online to existing face-to-face contacts (**Connections**)
■ Search out and connect to professional leaders (**Connections**)
■ Socialise and join conversations (**Conversations**)
■ Start to create new content (**Content**)

online environment is that there are many free online Web 2.0 tools to use. Some of these were covered in Chapter 3. I now outline the advantages of specific tools.

Web 2.0 tools for developing a personal brand

Blogging

The first obvious 'how to' marketing tool is blogging. Laurel Clyde's book on weblogs and libraries (2004) introduced me to blogs and since then, like many librarians, I have embraced blogging as one of my professional Web 2.0 tools. Why do I blog? Blogs are a useful way to record and reflect on learning. I started blogging while completing the 23 Things Learning 2.0 Programme, an online programme that introduced Web 2.0 technologies to libraries (Blowers, 2006). My blog provides me with an all-encompassing Web 2.0 platform where I share information about emerging technologies, photos, presentations, media and interact with colleagues about conferences and professional development activities.

Having a blog is a sure way to increase your online visibility. But blogging is not for everyone. In fact most blogs are abandoned within the first three years because many people just cannot keep them going. If you do start a blog, try to make a posting at least once a week. It is probably better not to have a blog at all than to have one that is incomplete or lapsed. If you want to start a blog, look into the free blog software options available. The main ones are Blogger, Wordpress and Typepad. The *advantages* of blogging for personal marketing are that it provides a place to create content, interact with others, and leverage your strengths in a way not possible in the offline world.

Squidoo

Writing online and adding online content is one way to build a positive online presence. A quick and easy way to do this is to use the community website Squidoo. With Squidoo you create pages (called 'lenses') on any subject of interest. The *advantages* of Squidoo are that it is easy to use and the platform caters for a wide range of media.

Google Profile

By simply creating an online profile, you can establish a web presence. Google offers many easy-to-use Web 2.0 tools: an RSS reader, alert software, a photo sharing site, start pages, blogging software, website building software to name a few. Google has a free profile product known as Google Profile, which the company describes thus:

> A Google profile is simply how you present yourself on Google products to other Google users. It allows you to control how you appear on Google and tell others a bit more about who you are. With a Google profile, you can easily share your web content on one central location. You can include, for example, links to your blog, online photos, and other profiles such as Facebook, LinkedIn, and more. You have control over what others see. Your profile won't display any private information unless you've explicitly added it. You can also allow people to find you more easily by enabling your profile to be searched by your name. Simply set your existing profile to show your full name publicly. (*http://www .google.com/accounts*)

Some advantages of using Google Profile are that you can use your Google Gmail account as login and then can link all your Google products together. Setting up a profile is simple and the profile is easy to use and greatly enhances your online visibility (see Figure 4.1). One personal branding feature is the customisable Google profile URL. You are able to use your name in the URL, which is an important feature. Now that so many people are on social networks, customisation of URLs with your name aids retrieval. Google Profile would be a good option if you did not already have your own blog. And even if you have a blog, Google Profile will bring everything in your Web 2.0 toolkit together and maximise your findability. As with all social networks, there are privacy concerns and Google has been accused of not taking enough care with users' privacy. Check Google's profile privacy settings to reassure yourself.

Figure 4.1   Google Profile

 Create your profile

What do people see when they find you online? You can control how you appear in Google by creating a personal profile...

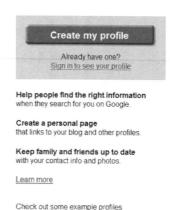

Create my profile

Already have one?
Sign in to see your profile

Help people find the right information when they search for you on Google.

Create a personal page
that links to your blog and other profiles.

Keep family and friends up to date
with your contact info and photos.

Learn more

Check out some example profiles

...and people will see it on their results page when they do web searches for your name.

SlideShare

If you do not have a blog, one way to get some of your professional ideas noticed is to share them on the social site,

SlideShare. You can do this even if you have never presented at a formal conference. If you are a student or an early-career professional, you may have had an opportunity to do a presentation during your studies. This could be adapted and distributed on SlideShare. For example, a presentation you made at a professional development seminar or workshop could provide a useful source of content.

SlideShare is similar to other social networking sites. On it you can search for LIS topics, 'follow' other people, choose favourites, form SlideShare groups and embed content on other sites. In the spirit of Web 2.0 openness, sharing and community, many web gurus share their content on SlideShare. SlideShare is also a great organisational tool, because you can store all your slides there. It lets you track who has viewed your slides and receive comments from them. The SlideShare widget also enables an RSS slide feed to be sent to your LinkedIn profile (RSS and widgets will be covered in Chapter 6). The advantages of SlideShare are the ease with which you can share content and connect with others without needing any particular web skills.

LinkedIn

LinkedIn provides a comprehensive platform for building a web presence and developing your own brand. Being much more comprehensive that Twitter, and more professional than Facebook, LinkedIn is one key tool that gives you a structure for showcasing your personal brand. You can enter the LinkedIn community at any stage in your career, from student through to early-career professional or professional leader.

Refer back to the LinkedIn areas I covered in Chapter 3. The advantages of LinkedIn for personal marketing are that it provides a professional context where you can leverage and integrate your content across different networks. Ensure that you use the summary section of the profile to include a strong statement of your achievements.

The examples of LinkedIn Summary profiles in Tables 4.2 and 4.3 show what could be concluded.

Table 4.2	Sample LinkedIn profile: LIS student

Sample LinkedIn profile
LIS student

Summary

I am a final year student in the Bachelor of Library and Information Science programme.

A highlight of my LIS studies has been having the opportunity to undertake library practicums which gave me experience in a variety of libraries: academic and public. I am passionate about libraries and the future of our profession. During my studies I worked on a marketing group project and used the latest Web 2.0 technology to develop a web presence for a public library 'meet the author' event. This project enabled me to further develop my strong interpersonal and communication skills. During my academic studies, I achieved the distinction of having my name on the 'Honour Roll' of the top 10 per cent of graduating students.

I am keen to develop my early career and have volunteered at the State Library and gained some experience in the Small Business collection. I am eager to establish myself in a library where I can use my talent and skills.

I am interested in softwares used in media and I have a special interest and skill using Adobe Photoshop. I am multilingual (English, Malay and Mandarin).

Specialties

Web 2.0, emerging technologies, marketing

Web 2.0 tools for eportfolios

As we have seen, LinkedIn provides an ideal Web 2.0 platform for developing a profile and marketing yourself.

Table 4.3	Sample LinkedIn profile: early-career professional

Sample LinkedIn profile
LIS early-career professional

Summary

I am a library and information professional with experience in public libraries. This is my second career. I was a history teacher before studying library and information science and moving into public libraries.

I am passionate about public libraries and working with the local community. I see great potential for libraries to work closer with community groups in digitising unique local collections.
Recent achievements include:

- developing a social network for the local community groups that use the public library
- starting a wiki for the early career networking group.

For the past two years I have helped library colleagues to organise a local public library conference. I am the secretary of the Local Library Conference Organising Committee and member of the LIS Early Career Mentoring Group.

Specialities

My specialities include social media applications for libraries, event planning, local history, leadership, interpersonal communication, time management and problem solving.

But you can go further than this and start to build an eportfolio, which would include documentary evidence of your work and achievements. A link to your eportfolio could then be included on LinkedIn as a way to enhance and strengthen your overall web presence. An eportfolio is an online space that you develop over time, providing a spot where potential employers can see your achievements. Eportfolios include a range of career-supporting materials and I list them further below.

Professional portfolios have been used in higher education for reflective learning and for showcasing and assessing students' work (Lorenzo and Ittelson, 2005; Hallam and

McAllister, 2008). They are also valuable tools for recording career achievements. Librarians have found eportfolios useful for keeping track of professional development and for marketing themselves (Hills et al., 2010). In the UK, portfolios form part of the chartership (accreditation) process for LIS professionals, managed through the Chartered Institute of Library and Information Professionals (CILIP).

In some higher education institutions students develop study-related eportfolios, using comprehensive, purpose-built software such as PebblePad (*http://www.pebblepad .co.uk/*) and Mahara (*http://mahara.org/*). However, you can develop an eportfolio using free Web 2.0 tools, as we will see. Such portfolios could range from the rudimentary to the more expansive.

Some librarian portfolio exemplars can be found in the list below, which was posted on the ALA LinkedIn Group by leading information consultant, Jill Hurst-Wahl (see *http:// www.hurstassociates.com/*):

- Kate Kosturski (portfolio): *http://www.katekosturski.com/*

- Fiona Bradley (portfolio): *http://www.fionabradley.com/*

- Lori Satter (portfolio): *http://www.lorisatter.com/*

- Megan Oakleaf (portfolio): *http://www.meganoakleaf .info/*

- Kathryn Greenhill (portfolio): *http://kathryngreenhill .com/*

- E. Shander Bowden (portfolio): *http://www.hoboy.net/ shander/*

These examples show a variety of approaches and softwares and are useful to guide you in developing an eportfolio of your own.

Susanne Markgren (2010) suggests using free software such as PBWorks, WordPress or Google Sites. PBWorks *(http://pbworks.com/)* is actually a collaborative wiki tool, but it can also be used for eportfolios. It has some advantages: (1) it offers a simple to use interface for beginners; (2) it allows you to incorporate Word documents, PDFs and other media; (3) it is free for the basic PBWorks service.

Some examples of portfolios developed on PBWorks are:

■ Susanne Markgren (portfolio): *http://smportfolio.pbworks .com/*

■ Julia Gross (portfolio): *http://jaygee.pbworks.com/*

While these Web 2.0 tools mentioned above do not offer the same functionality as purpose-built portfolio software such as PebblePad or Mahara, they are perfectly adequate for getting started.

What to include in a portfolio would depend on who you are and your career needs. Some examples are:

■ a brief biography and contact details;

■ your curriculum vitae or résumé;

■ documents, such as lists of your projects and achievements;

■ lists of professional development courses attended and workshops completed;

■ online examples of your work, such as videos or presentations;

■ links to your publications or written work;

■ links to your social networking profiles.

Twitter

Twitter can also be used to develop your personal brand. The barrier to entry for Twitter is not great, so even if you do nothing else, give Twitter a try. Twitter is used by many as a recreational social network, but having a web presence on Twitter that is about you as a LIS professional can be invaluable. Some people choose to keep two Twitter accounts, one recreational and one professional, but I really do not think this is necessary. So long as you are careful with what you post, it can be quite advantageous to blend personal and professional postings. The blended Twitter approach shows others your fun side as well as your professional side.

There are a number of dos and don'ts in using Twitter professionally:

- Do not lock your Twitter account and make it private. It will put others off from finding and following you and will defeat the purpose of having greater online visibility.

- Make use of the brief biographical section and include some relevant information about yourself.

- In the Twitter profile section add a link to your website or blog. You have only one option here, so make it something impressive. If you don't have a blog or website, then provide a link to your LinkedIn profile or your Google profile.

- Add a photo or image. Twitter is one social network where use of an avatar image rather than your photo in your profile is quite acceptable. Do not use the Twitter default image because this would indicate you are not a serious or professional Twitterer.

- Follow some of the LIS leading professionals and join in a conversation.

- Help others with information and be sociable; this is the essence of *social* networks.

- Include in your tweets links to interesting professional news, blog posts and the like.

- Once you have been on Twitter for a while you can boost your online presence by becoming proactive and creating your own Twitter list (i.e. list of fellow Twitterers who tweet on similar topics). You may then be listed by others and your network will increase.

■ Amplify your Twitter activity by integrating it with the other social networking sites you use. For example, Twitter can be integrated with Facebook, LinkedIn and other social media sites, so that particular tweets can be distributed on these networks. You need to check the networks' connection settings to see how this is done and then code your tweets with: #fb for Facebook, and/or #in for LinkedIn.

■ Try live tweeting an event, such as a library conference, via your laptop, mobile phone or iPad. (Many conferences provide free WiFi.) This will certainly bring you new followers and raise your online profile.

■ Follow the Twitter hash tag to participate in a remote conference on the other side of the world. You could comment on interesting news, conference papers, and retweet useful information. This connects you to the Twittersphere and boosts your web presence in ways that would have been unimaginable several years ago. Conference Twitter hash tags are usually posted on the conference website or blog. (There is more about conferences and Twitter in Chapter 7.)

Importance and benefits of marketing

Clearly there are many reasons why marketing is important. If you want your career to be successful, you need to:

■ prove your worth;

■ explain to others what you do, even if you are not currently job seeking;

- compete for jobs and opportunities within the workplace;
- differentiate yourself in the job marketplace;
- make sure your strengths and capabilities are understood and recognised.

Caveat

With online presence being linked to careers there is a lot at stake now, which leads us to ponder how you can establish your bona fides in the online world. Behave in the online world as you would face to face and be genuine in what you write. Do not be tempted to embellish the truth. Your online presence supports your personal, face-to-face career efforts and does not replace them.

Conclusion

In this chapter I have presented several ways for you to build an online presence. I strongly advise that you do *not* need to action *all* of these. The range is provided here to show what is possible and what can work. Depending on where you are in the career journey, some of these Web 2.0 tools will fit your situation better than others. Trying to do all this at once could be overwhelming.

Start with small steps and build your presence over time. For example, if you feel blogging is not for you then stick to Twitter, or LinkedIn or sharing slide content on SlideShare. Think about your online presence in terms of setting short-term and long-term goals.

As mentioned above, once you have developed an online brand by using some of these Web 2.0 tools, you can enhance it by adding a link to your eportfolio.

There are some marketing books available on how to market libraries and library services, but few on how to market ourselves. Many library career development books have chapters on personal marketing: see the Reference list and URLs at the end of the chapter. And read some of the experts in the field of the LIS personal brand: Mary Ellen Bates, Kim Dority and Scott Brown.

Once you have recognised that using Web 2.0 tools gives you greater online visibility, you are well on the way to understanding that social media can help you build an online identity that serves your career. In Chapter 5, I introduce the concept of the digital footprint and the privacy implications of having increased web visibility.

References

Bates, M.E. (2003) Marketing on the Web. In M.E. Bates and R. Basch, *Building & Running a Successful Research Business: A Guide for the Independent Information Professional* (pp. 245–57). Medford, NJ: CyberAge Books.

Blowers, H. (2006) *Learning 2.0* (blog). Retrieved 1 March 2007, from *http://plcmclearning.blogspot.com/*.

Clyde, L.A. (2004) *Weblogs and Libraries*. Oxford: Chandos.

Dority, K.G. (2006) *Rethinking Information Work: A Career Guide for Librarians and Other Information Professionals*. Westport, CN: Libraries Unlimited.

Hallam, G.C. and McAllister, L.M. (2008) *Self Discovery through Digital Portfolios: a Holistic Approach to Developing New Library and Information Professionals*. Paper presented at the Digital discovery: strategies and solutions: 29th Annual Conference of the International Association of Technological University Libraries (IATUL), Auckland,

New Zealand. *http://eprints.qut.edu.au/14048/1/14048 .pdf.*

Hills, C., Randle, R. and Beazley, J. (2010) *ePortfolios a Plan for Success: Australian New Graduate Experiences.* Paper presented at the IFLA 2010 Open access to knowledge – promoting sustainable progress, Gothenburg, Sweden. Retrieved 2 December 2010, from *http://www/ifla.org/en/ ifla76.*

Lorenzo, G. and Ittelson, J. (2005) *An Overview of e-Portfolios. Educause.* Retrieved 2 December, 2010, from *http://net.educause.edu/ir/library/pdf/ELI3001.pdf.*

Markgren, S. (2010) *Using Portfolios and Profiles to Professionalize your Online Identity (for free).* Retrieved 2 December 2010, from *http://www.liscareer.com/markgren_ portfolio.htm.*

OCLC (2007) *Sharing, Privacy and Trust in our Networked World: A Report to the OCLC Membership.* Dublin, OH: OCLC.

Rossiter, N. (2008) *Marketing the Best Deal in Town: Your Library: Where is Your Purple Owl?* Oxford: Chandos.

Useful weblinks

Bates, Mary Ellen. Brand you and Web 2.0, SLA Annual conference, June 2010: *http://www.batesinfo.com/extras/ index_assets/SLA-Brand-You.pdf*

Brown, Scott. Your personal brand and social media, SLA Annual conference, June 2010: *http://www.slideshare.net/ scbrown5/sla-social-brandingjune2010final*

Dority, Kim G. LinkedIn: Everything I ever wanted to tell you, but was too shy/modest/embarrassed to say. *http:// www.liscareer.com/dority_linkedin.htm*

Google Profile: *http://www.google.com/accounts*

Google Sites: *http://sites.google.com*

Hansen, Randall S. Quintessential careers: *http://www*
.quintcareers.com/jobseeker_marketing_tools.html

Krosski, Ellyssa. Workshop how to create an online presence:
http://oedb.org/blogs/ilibrarian/2010/workshop-how-to-
create-an-online-presence/

Mahara: *http://mahara.org/*

PBWorks: *http://pbworks.com/*

PebblePad: *http://www.pebblepad.co.uk/*

SlideShare home: *http://www.slideshare.net/*

Socialmediatoday.com: *http://socialmediatoday.com/mattam*
brose/144596/how-social-media-can-help-graduates-
build-their-personal-brand-and-get-job

Squidoo: *http://www.squidoo.com/*

Wordpress: *http://wordpress.com/*

5

Privacy, social networking and your career

Abstract: This chapter focuses on the problem of privacy in the Web 2.0 world. It examines the history of the slow erosion of online privacy since the early days of the Internet and investigates current research on the topic of changing generational attitudes to privacy. The chapter emphasises the risks LIS professionals need to consider in relation to online privacy and their career. It also describes the useful concept of the digital footprint and provides techniques and tools for monitoring your footprint. To sum up: the chapter provides answers to common questions that arise with social networking and privacy, and it also includes a list of sources that provide advice and *actions that can be taken to ameliorate risks to privacy.*

Key words: career, Web 2.0, LIS professionals, librarians, privacy, social networking sites, digital footprint, web presence, Facebook, Google Alerts.

I have stated in previous chapters that participating in Web 2.0 communities presents us with a thorny question: how can we maintain control over our privacy? The glib answer to this question would be that we cannot, because Web 2.0 involves openness and sharing. Admittedly, it does appear that attitudes to privacy are changing and that it is somewhat acceptable to reveal more personal information than in the past. Additionally, concerns about privacy may be different across generations. If so, this would indicate a permanent shift is under way. Nevertheless, the privacy issue continues to cause unease because of the perceived lack of control and the actual lack of understanding of the new online social norms. Therefore, privacy demands our attention, and in this chapter I examine some of the issues it raises.

In Chapter 3 I discussed how social networking sites, such as Facebook and Twitter, are blurring the boundaries between public and private online spaces. And in Chapter 4 I encouraged you to establish a positive online presence and build a brand identity using Web 2.0 technologies. All of these steps in establishing an online presence to support your career goals lead to you revealing more about your private self than you may otherwise have done.

In this chapter I present current research on privacy and Web 2.0 and describe techniques and tools for investigating your digital footprint. Finally, I provide practical solutions and sources to help you manage privacy pitfalls and avoid problems in the future.

Some of the questions that may arise about online privacy are:

- Why is privacy important?
- What has changed to make online privacy an issue now?
- Are there generational differences in attitudes to privacy?
- Who is responsible for ensuring online privacy?
- What is the history of privacy erosion in the online world?

I will now endeavour to deal with these questions, particularly as they relate to your career and professional reputation.

Why is privacy important?

Privacy is important because it is an area of online interactions where the status quo is being significantly challenged. In the past individuals have been used to having some control over what information was private. What is so special about being private? As danah boyd explains:

> Privacy is a sense of control over information, the context where sharing takes place, and the audience who can gain access. Information is not private because no one knows it; it is private because the knowing is limited and controlled. In most scenarios, the limitations are often more social than structural. (boyd, 2008)

For the sake of your career you need to know about the privacy issues, and know how to put checks and balances in place.

What has changed to make online privacy an issue now?

It used to be that some of our personal communication could be private and controlled to a large extent (barring any breaches of confidence). Personal communication may have consisted of a face-to-face meeting, a phone conversation, or private written communication. We would have been aggrieved if a switchboard operator listened in to our phone conversation or someone in the mail room opened our letters. There were boundaries, as boyd explains, including spatial boundaries, such as buildings, or limited audio range. Even in public spaces we had a sense of being able to create a private space within. But rapid changes have occurred because the emergence of Web 2.0 has been accompanied by a convergence of the private and public online social worlds. In the eyes of leading new media researcher, danah boyd, this has led to what she terms 'social convergence' and a collapse of 'discrete social contexts'. She elucidates further:

> Media and technological convergence are introducing new practices and opportunities. Yet, as a direct result of these structural changes, another form of convergence is emerging: social convergence. Social convergence occurs when disparate social contexts are collapsed into one ... social convergence requires people to handle disparate audiences simultaneously without a social script. (boyd, 2008)

The social convergence that boyd talks about helps to explain why some users of social media feel a sense of unease regarding privacy and doubt that social media network owners can be trusted to keep personal information private. Undoubtedly, social norms of online communication are changing and, as a consequence, some people feel they have lost control of the situation. Is this a transitional stage in public attitudes to privacy? Will the next generation adjust to the new norms, or will there be a privacy backlash? These, of course, are questions that will take some time to be answered. But for the present, there are some recent studies about attitudinal change that might help us to make some predictions.

Are there generational differences in attitudes to privacy?

It has been claimed that the majority of complaints about loss of privacy have been voiced by an older cohort of social media users and that teenagers' attitudes to privacy are different. It is important to investigate this hypothesis. If true, there may be a fundamental change taking place that may later spread across generations. If not true, then the right to privacy needs to be more vigorously asserted.

What evidence is there of generational differences in attitudes to privacy? danah boyd is critical of claims that teenagers do not care about privacy:

> There's an assumption that teens don't care about privacy but this is completely inaccurate. Teens care deeply about privacy, but their conceptualization of what this means may not make sense in a setting where privacy settings are a binary. What teens care about is the ability to control information as it flows and to have the information necessary to adjust to a situation when information flows too far or in unexpected ways....they (teens) are highlighting that both privacy AND publicity have value. (boyd, 2010)

The PEW Research Center report, 'Reputation management and social media' (Madden and Smith, 2010) found that younger users of social media sites cared enough about their personal data to actively go in and alter privacy settings. Specifically, the research found younger users to be more vigilant in controlling privacy, as Tables 5.1 and 5.2 indicate.

Table 5.1 Percentage of Internet users who altered privacy settings on social networking sites

Age group	Percentage
18–29 year olds	71
30–49 year olds	62
50–64 year olds	55

Source: Madden and Smith (2010)

| Table 5.2 | Percentage of Internet users who took steps to limit personal information available on social networking sites |

Age group	Percentage
18–29 year olds	44
30–49 year olds	33
50–64 year olds	20

Source: Madden and Smith (2010)

This data indicates that younger users were not cavalier about privacy matters; in fact they were more inclined to control access to certain parts of their personal information.

Another study from the Pew Research Center to throw some light on generational attitudes to privacy is 'Millennials will make online sharing in networks a lifelong habit' (Anderson and Rainie, 2010). This study found that Millennials (those born between 1980 and 1995) who were early adopters of social media may be less likely to have concerns about privacy. It should be pointed out that the user group (895 Internet experts) surveyed were a non-random online sample, recruited via e-mail invitation, and therefore not representative of the population at large. One of the findings of the survey was that some respondents felt that, in relation to privacy and openness:

> an awkward trial-and-error period is unfolding and will continue over the next decade, as people adjust to new realities about how social networks perform and as new boundaries are set about the personal information that is appropriate to share. (Anderson and Rainie, 2010)

So it would appear from the research that some attitudinal changes to privacy are taking place.

Who is responsible for ensuring online privacy?

The right to privacy, including the control of access to information about citizens, is enshrined in law in many democratic countries. Privacy laws are different in different countries and it is far beyond the scope of this book to cover privacy law. Privacy breaches in relation to social networking are proving to be a challenge to law makers, and some experts say that privacy laws have not caught up with the rapid growth and diversity in online communities.

First you need to find out what privacy laws apply to online social networking in your country. For example in Australia, the Privacy Act regulates 'information privacy'. Also, there is an Australian Government Privacy Commissioner, whose role is to pursue breaches of privacy law. Some other English-speaking countries have similar arrangements. At the end of the chapter I have listed some agencies that provide assistance in, and information about, privacy law in several countries. One important point to note is that the privacy laws of your country may not reach beyond national boundaries.

Each of us needs to inform ourselves of online privacy and decide where we stand. As danah boyd states:

> Privacy is not an inalienable right – it is a privilege that must be protected socially and structurally in order to exist. The question remains as to whether or not privacy is something that society wishes to support. (boyd, 2008)

Further on in this chapter, I provide actions you can take to protect your privacy online.

What is the history of privacy erosion in the online world?

In the early days of the Internet there was much debate about online identity and whether one could or should remain anonymous when online. The famous 1993 *New Yorker* cartoon of a dog typing into a computer, with the accompanying caption: 'on the Internet, nobody knows you're a dog', was illustrative of the thinking at the time. Back then, our identity could be somewhat hidden and our privacy maintained to some extent. What has changed? One change has been that control has been slipping away as we have shared more information online. This is happening relentlessly, and maybe we have not really been aware of its happening.

danah boyd (2008) outlines a brief history of the Internet and privacy from the 1990s onwards and she shows that there has been a slow erosion of online privacy involving a range of companies from DejaNews to Yahoo! And the Internet community has had concerns about online privacy since the 1990s. With Web 2.0 the online social space is more complex, less controlled and less private.

Privacy and your career

Breaches of privacy can have a direct impact on your career. In Chapter 1, I discussed the results of the 2009 CareerBuilder.com survey that showed employers are using social-networking sites to discover information about job applicants. This trend is growing, as data on the CareerBuilder website indicates. I pointed out in Chapter 1 that we should not think of this as just a negative, and in Chapter 4

84

I discussed online identity and showed that increased online visibility can work in your favour if you are proactive and present a positive online image to a prospective employer. However, errors of judgement have been made and many instances have been reported in the media.

Employee–privacy case studies

There have been numerous misadventures experienced by employees and employers on the social networks. I will outline just a few here, to illustrate what can go wrong.

Cisco Fatty

The following Twitter exchange in March 2009 – known as the 'Cisco Fatty' incident – has become legendary (Duffy, 2009).

This message was posted on Twitter by a prospective Cisco employee:

> Cisco just offered me a job! Now I have to weigh the utility of a fatty paycheck against the daily commute to San Jose and hating the work.

This response came from a Cisco employee who saw the message on Twitter:

> Who is the hiring manager? I'm sure they would love to know that you will hate the work. We here at Cisco are versed in the web.

Facebook 'boring' job gaffe

A young employee was dismissed, after making a comment on Facebook about her job being 'boring'.

> 'Teenage office worker Kimberley Swann was sacked from her job after branding it "boring" on Facebook' (Telegraph. co.uk, 2010)

The above examples illustrate stupid mistakes made by individuals online. It may well be that the media is exaggerating the risk and that some prospective employers will be lenient towards such misjudgements, but my advice would be: do not take the risk.

Having your online identity subverted and distorted in some way is a far more serious breach of privacy. Such attacks border on cybercrime because they can do serious harm and damage to reputations. In the section below, on how to monitor your digital footprint, I have included some tips for spotting such occurrences, which fortunately are not common. In the privacy FAQ below (from the Australian Privacy Commissioner) I have provided a summary of their advice and suggested actions.

Privacy and Facebook

In Chapter 3, I provided a snapshot of Facebook's growth from the Harvard campus in 2004 to the present day. Facebook has continually pushed the boundaries on privacy by making changes to their default settings and introducing more open features. In 2008 in an article titled, 'Facebook's privacy trainwreck', danah boyd described the steady erosion of privacy on the network. But why has Facebook been singled out for criticism when Twitter and LinkedIn provide even less privacy? There are three reasons. First, the size of the Facebook network is huge (500 million members by mid-2010) and growing, so any privacy change they make affects many people. Second, Facebook members represent a wide demographic that includes many users who are less savvy in making technical changes required to remain more private. Third, Facebook was set up from the beginning as a more self-contained private type of network.

Mark Zuckerberg, the founder of Facebook, believes that making more personal information public is acceptable, particularly among Millennials. In an interview in January 2010 (reported by Marshall Kirkpatrick of Read Write Web), Zuckerberg stated:

> People have really gotten comfortable not only sharing more information and different kinds, but more openly and with more people. That social norm is just something that has evolved over time. (Kirkpatrick, 2010)

To sum up, Facebook has been slowly weakening their default privacy settings and has lost the trust of some members.

Privacy and Google

Facebook has been singled out for scrutiny, but Google also has privacy problems. In July 2010 Google broke Australian privacy law when it mistakenly collected private information from local Wi-Fi networks. This occurred while the company was collecting data for the mapping service, Google Street View. For some, Street View has proved to be an unwelcome intrusion on privacy and Google is being challenged over it in many countries:

> The privacy breaches occurred in 30 countries, including Australia. It [Google] is facing a class action suit in

the U.S. over the Street View snooping. (Foo, 9 July, 2010)

I now turn my attention to some actions you can take to investigate and monitor your web presence and control your privacy.

Digital footprint

A key concept for understanding the shifts taking place in privacy online is the digital footprint, that is the consequences of your activities and behaviours online and the size of your web presence. The more active you are online the larger will be your digital footprint. As you move around various sites you leave digital tracks or footprints. And in terms of your career, you should be starting to think about the positives and negatives of your footprint. You have a footprint by simply joining a website, posting to blogs, releasing any personal information online, and by even just connecting to the Internet. Your existing footprint may be a result of something active you have done, such as establishing your brand, which I promoted in Chapters 3 and 4. And it could be something passive such as your name being mentioned on a social networking site, or your photo being posted without your knowledge. I will discuss this below.

Some other activities that contribute to your digital footprint are:

- bookmarking sites on the net;
- setting up your own website or blog;
- using social networking sites: Twitter, Facebook, LinkedIn and others.

You can now begin to monitor changes to your footprint.

How to monitor your digital footprint

Once you recognise that you already have a digital footprint, you can check and begin to monitor it. In the marketing and social media business, this is becoming a common practice. It is known as 'brand monitoring' or 'reputation management'.

The PEW Research Center report, 'Reputation management and social media' (Madden and Smith, 2010), reports that experienced social media users are increasingly monitoring their digital footprint. The PEW surveys conducted in 2006 and 2009 confirm this trend (see Table 5.3).

How is monitoring done? The easiest way is to search for your name in a search engine, such as Google and in Google images. This is a useful exercise to establish what is already online under your name.

Google Alerts

Once you have conducted a Google search on your name, you can set up a Google Alert on that search. Then Google Alerts will send you an automated e-mail message letting you know when new information has been found. The updated information is retrieved from blogs, news stories and web pages. These alerts are similar to the journal or database alerts that librarians often advise their clients on.

Table 5.3	Percentage of Internet users who took steps to monitor their digital footprint	

Year	Percentage
2006	47
2009	57

Source: Madden and Smith (2010)

To set up an alert on your name, go to the Google Alerts URL *www.google.com/alerts* and take the following steps:

1. Enter your name as a query.
2. Include everything you wish to be searched (news, blogs, video etc.).
3. State how often you want the update to appear.
4. State how long the e-mail message should be (you can set a limit).
5. Provide your e-mail address (Google Gmail).

Soon you will receive a verification e-mail back from Google and subsequently, when there are new results, Google Alerts sends them to you in an e-mail. You can later go into your Google Gmail account to manage, edit, or change the alerts. For example, you can change the delivery method from e-mail to RSS. I will be discussing RSS and setting up RSS feeds in Chapter 6.

Once you have set up an alert, you should carry out regular 'housekeeping' and track activity around your footprint. In Chapter 10 I provide a section on housekeeping – organising all your online accounts and keeping track of your alerts, RSS feeds and passwords.

FAQs and actions for online privacy

I discussed above the sense of loss of control over information that some feel with privacy. Who is responsible for ensuring online privacy? There are laws and agencies to guide us, but in the end we all need to assert some control over our online information, where we can. Danah boyd says: 'It used to take effort to be public. Today, it often takes effort to be private' (2010).

Do not assume that the default privacy settings on social networking sites are sufficient. In the remaining part of this chapter, I will provide some steps to help you take a more rigorous approach to privacy, guided by advice from the Australian Government Office of the Australian Information Commissioner. There are a number of government privacy information websites around the world, some of which I have listed below.

The website of the Office of the Australian Information Commissioner (*http://www.oaic.gov.au/*) posts a list of frequently asked questions (an FAQ) in relation to social networking and privacy. I have paraphrased these questions and responses and present them below:

1. *Are there any privacy risks associated with using social networking sites?*

    ■ Yes, but you can take steps to minimise the risks.

    ■ Be aware it may not just be friends listening in.

    ■ Think before you post: would you be comfortable with your employer seeing your message and/or photos?

    ■ Send any private message to friends as direct message or e-mail.

    ■ Social networking sites can feel like a private spaces, but they are not.

    ■ Remember that you are responsible for the privacy of friends and family.

    ■ Do not reveal phone numbers or addresses; identity thieves can use your personal information.

2. *Are organisations allowed to use the personal information I post on social networking sites?*

    ■ Potential employers could *look* at your information.

    ■ Commercial use is governed by laws.

3. *What can I do to protect my privacy when using social networking sites?*

   ■ Read the privacy policy regularly.

   ■ Use the privacy tools available.

4. *How long does my information stay on social networking sites?*

   ■ A long time – it can live on in archived versions of the site.

5. *Do I have rights under the Privacy Act when I use social networking sites?*

   ■ Possibly *not*, if the social networking site is based in another country.

6. *If I have a privacy-related complaint about a social networking site, who can I complain to?*

   ■ Contact the site.

   ■ Complain to the trust-mark issuer, if there is one listed on the site.

7. *What can I do if someone posts information about me on a social networking site that I want removed?*

   ■ Ask the person to take it down.

   ■ Contact the site as most sites have grievance proce-dures.

8. *What can I do if I'm being threatened, harassed or defamed online?*

   ■ Take immediate action and, if necessary, contact the police. (*http://www.privacy.gov.au/faq/individualsIcial_networking*).

Government agencies providing support for privacy

Many countries have agencies and privacy commissioners' websites that provide FAQs and contact points for responding to privacy questions from the public. Some have particular support for privacy and social networking, because this is an emerging area of concern. These are some that may cover your region:

- Office of the Australian Information Commissioner: *http:// www.oaic.gov.au/*

- Canadian Office of the Privacy Commissioner: information and a number of resources about social networking sites are available on its website: *http://www.priv.gc.ca/ resource/ii_5_01_e.cfmc/ontenttop*

- New Zealand Privacy Commissioner: *http://www.privacy .org.nz/*

- Ontario Office of the Privacy Commissioner (Canada): a number of resources about social networking sites are available on its website, including: *http://www.ipc.on.ca/ english/Home-Page/*

- Ontario Office of the Privacy Commissioner (Canada). Reference check: is your boss watching? Privacy and your Facebook profile: *http://www.ipc.on.ca/images/Resources/ facebook-refcheck.pdf*

- UK Information Commissioner's Office: includes a site for young people that gives information about social networking sites and how to protect your privacy online: *http://www.ico.gov.uk/youth.aspx*

- USA EPIC is a public interest research centre in Washington, DC. It was established in 1994 to focus public attention on emerging civil liberties issues and to protect privacy, the First Amendment, and constitutional values: *http:// epic.org/*

- USA OnGuard Online: provides practical tips to help protect your personal information online, secure computers and guard against Internet fraud: *http://www .onguardonline.gov/topics/social-networking-sites.aspx*

Tracking privacy changes on social networking sites

You need to be vigilant to keep up to date with current news about privacy and Web 2.0. Changes in privacy settings may be announced when you log in to a social networking site and the implications may not be immediately obvious. Frequently the default will amount to *less* privacy unless you take action and alter the default privacy settings. And, as we have seen with Facebook, making changes to their privacy settings can be convoluted and difficult to understand.

The blogs and websites that are devoted to discussing social media frequently contain current information on privacy. They provide the best way to keep track of social media privacy changes, and often provide videos or step-by-step guides to making adjustments to privacy settings. Worthwhile social media blogs and websites for privacy discussions are:

- Electronic Frontier Foundation (EFF): *http://www.eff.org/*
- Mashable (blog): *http://mashable.com/*
- Read Write Web (blog): *http://www.readwriteweb.com/*
- ReputationDefender Blog: *http://www.reputationdefender blog.com/*

All of these sites provide a search function. You should search under 'privacy' to find all the relevant entries. The

Reputation Defender site listed above offers a specific service that will check your exposure to online privacy and reputation risks.

Conclusion

In this chapter my goal has been to shine some light on the difficult area of online privacy. Social media is pushing many of us out of our privacy comfort zones, where new norms of behaviour prevail. Online media and privacy expert danah boyd describes this as social convergence where the boundaries between public and private are blurred. There will always be a tension between wishing to join the online conversation and having concerns about the risk of revealing too much. However, it is important to ponder these issues and plan to ameliorate the risks. In this chapter I have discussed the notion of the digital footprint. If you know what your footprint is, you can start to proactively check your footprint and monitor any problems or issues that may arise.

The Web 2.0 technologies provide you with many career opportunities, and you need to weigh up the benefits versus the privacy risks. As users of Web 2.0, we need to make decisions about our online privacy. Yes, privacy can present problems. But these are problems that all users of the Internet confront; we can and should manage them ourselves.

References

Anderson, J. and Rainie, L. (2010) *Millennials Will Make Online Sharing in Networks a Lifelong Habit.* Pew Internet & American Life Project, 9 July 2010. Retrieved 1 August 2010, from *http://pewinternet.org/Reports/2010/ Future-of-Millennials.aspx.*

Betancourt, L. (2009) *Protecting Online Identity. Mashable*. Retrieved 25 August 2010, from *http://mashable.com/2009/04/21/protecting-online-identity/*.

boyd, d. (2008) Facebook's Privacy Trainwreck: Exposure, Invasion, and Social Convergence. *Convergence,* 14(1).

boyd, d. (2010) *Public by Default, Private When Necessary*. Retrieved 25 August 2010, from *http://www.zephoria.org/thoughts/archives/2010/01/25/public_by_defau.html*.

boyd, d. and Hargittai, E. (2010) Facebook privacy settings: Who cares? *First Monday,* 15(8).

Duffy, J. (2009) Tweeted out of a job: The 'Cisco Fatty' story. *Network World* (blog). Retrieved 25 August 2010, from *http://www.networkworld.com/community/node/39874.*

Fletcher, D. (2010) How Facebook is redefining privacy. *Time,* 175(21), 1.

Foo, F. (2010) Google Australia breached Privacy Act with Street View but escapes with apology. *The Australian.* Retrieved from *http://www.theaustralian.com.au/australian-it/google-australia-breached-privacy-act-but-apology-is-sufficient/story-e6frgakx-1225889876666.*

Kirkpatrick, M. (2010) Facebook's Zuckerberg says the age of privacy is over. *Read Write Web* (blog). Retrieved 25 August 2010, from *http://www.readwriteweb.com/archives/facebooks_zuckerberg_says_the_age_of_privacy_is_ov.php.*

Madden, M. and Smith, A. (2010) *Reputation Management and Social Media: How People Monitor their Identity and Search for Others Online*. Pew Internet & American Life Project, 26 May 2010. Retrieved 13 September 2010, from *http://www.pewinternet.org/Reports/2010/Reputation-Management.aspx.*

Steiner, P. (1993) On the internet, nobody knows you're a dog (cartoon), *New Yorker* p. 61.

Telegraph.co.uk. (2010) *Top 10 Gaffes on Facebook, Twitter and Google.* Retrieved 15 September 2010, from *http://www.telegraph.co.uk/technology/facebook/7635982/Top-10-gaffes-on-Facebook-Twitter-and-Google.html.*

Weinberg, T. (2008) Manage your online reputation. *Lifehacker.* Retrieved 25 August 2010, from *http://lifehacker.com/357460/manage-your-online-reputation.*

Useful weblinks

CareerBuilder.com: *http://www.careerbuilder.com/*
Google Alerts: *http://www.google.com/alerts*
Office of the Australian Information Commissioner: *http://www.oaic.gov.au/*
Wikipedia.Privacylaw:*http://en.wikipedia.org/wiki/Privacy_law*

6

Lifelong learning
and your career

Abstract: This chapter deals with the lifelong learning imperative for LIS professionals. It highlights the need for LIS professionals to embrace lifelong learning throughout their careers. The chapter provides an overview of how career paths are changing and of the new roles that are emerging in libraries. It outlines strategies for becoming a lifelong learner. The chapter focuses on some Web 2.0 technologies that support lifelong learning, in particular how RSS can be used as a tool to support lifelong learning by managing and controlling the information flow.

Key words: Career, Web 2.0, LIS professionals, librarians, lifelong learning, RSS, Google Reader, start pages, iGoogle, Netvibes, Yahoo! Pipes.

Thirty or forty years ago when we entered a chosen career we expected it to last a lifetime. This is certainly no longer the case. As a result of constant change, career paths can be transitory. Many professionals will change careers two or three times during their working lives. Some may have come into LIS as a second career. Within the LIS field, new roles are emerging and there are synergies with some related professions. Now, even if you stay in the same career area for a time, some of the knowledge you acquired during your course of studies will become obsolete. In some disciplines, particularly those in the technology areas, the 'shelf life' of a degree may be quite short – barely a few years. Because library and information careers are driven increasingly by rapid technological change, LIS professionals need to keep up with trends and take responsibility for their own lifelong learning.

In Chapter 1, I outlined the *three cornerstones* of career activities: marketing, networking and professional development, and throughout the book I have dealt with these topics and introduced Web 2.0 technologies that may assist you to reach your career goals. This chapter deals with lifelong learning – learning with and about Web 2.0 technologies. I highlight some tools you can explore independently. Subsequently, in Chapter 7, I deal with continuing professional development. The remaining chapters in the book follow on with the theme of lifelong learning: Chapter 9 on mentoring and Chapter 10 on keeping up to date.

Career paths and new roles in LIS

Career researchers recognise that the logical progression that 'career path' implies is not matched by reality: careers may not necessarily be linear, but can evolve rather more chaotically (Bloch, 2004). The career progression that you hope and plan for may, for various reasons, never eventuate. There are unpredictable external factors that impact on careers, such as the global economy and organisational change. There are internal factors too, such as changing personal and family circumstances, that will also impact on your career plans.

New roles are emerging in libraries, the nature of which may not yet be clear. MacLennan (2004) talks about the process of 'becoming' a librarian throughout one's working life. She says that librarians are:

embarking on a career trajectory that unfolds continuously into a sequence of changes and opportunities that can lead in many different career paths. Librarians are continually 'becoming' or metamorphosing into new areas, into multifaceted dimensions of the information realm. (MacLennan, 2004)

These new roles and areas will vary depending on what sector you work in or aim to work in. For example, the notion of the 'embedded librarian', working with a team of researchers, is being proposed in some research library settings (Shumaker, 2010). In universities, some library roles are becoming more aligned to teaching, learning and research (Webb et al., 2007). To be in a position to take advantage of new roles and opportunities that may arise, you need to be abreast of trends and be an independent learner. Whether you are an early-career, mid-career or late-career librarian, your employment prospects will be boosted if you can demonstrate you are up to date with professional issues. Do not assume that your course of study has taught all you need to know. If you are in the workforce, some learning opportunities may be provided by your employer. However, you cannot afford to sit back and hope that this will happen. Besides, the workplace training that is offered may not be targeted to emerging library and information trends. Becoming a lifelong learner is critical for LIS professionals working in the knowledge economy.

What is lifelong learning?

Lifelong learning is an all-encompassing, commonly used term that is in danger of becoming a cliché. The term incorporates the idea of individual achievement. It also includes elements of skill and knowledge acquisition and of individuals having an aptitude and a desire to learn and grow. It is difficult to come up with an exact definition of lifelong learning because it is not a settled concept – such terms are always contested. However, one definition that fits my general purpose is this:

> Lifelong learning is the development of human potential through a continuously supportive process which stimulates and empowers individuals to acquire all the knowledge, values, skills, and understanding they will require throughout their lifetimes and to apply them with confidence, creativity and enjoyment in all roles, circumstances, and environments. (Longworth and Davies, 1996)

Lifelong learning has elements of adult education, continuing education, self-directed learning, and the ideal of the individual reaching his/her full potential. There have been global initiatives towards lifelong learning and education for the whole life span, dating back to the 1990s. Governments in Europe and the United States have supported lifelong learning as an ideal means to facilitate global competition in the knowledge-based economies. (Maehl, 2003)

Lifelong learning and student graduate attributes

Currently, a commitment to lifelong learning underpins courses in many higher education institutions. This is being driven by several factors, including a recognition that graduates need to be equipped with particular skills and attributes to adapt to the workplace. In some academic institutions, lifelong learning is identified in the curriculum as a graduate attribute. In these institutions all students are expected to graduate with an orientation towards lifelong learning. As Hallam and McAllister put it:

> Employer bodies stress the need for graduates who are ready to 'hit the ground running', to be equipped with a skill set that encompasses the discipline knowledge as well as the personal attributes that are required in the workplace. (Hallam and McAllister, 2008)

In this era of the 'crowded curriculum', when there is too much content to cover in too short a time, university and college students who acquire some independence in their learning are well on their way to becoming lifelong learners. Ideally, those students who acquire attributes towards learning will continue to be learners in the workplace.

Strategies for becoming a lifelong learner

What can you do to become an independent lifelong learner? Perhaps the first step is to realise that becoming a lifelong learner is as much about developing a curiosity and a thirst for learning as it is about acquiring particular skills. However, there are some tangible strategies and actions that you can take to set you on this path:

- Join the professional association and learn from colleagues.
- Attend professional development seminars and conferences.
- Seek out mentors in the profession.

- Keep up with professional reading.
- Think about starting a blog to record your learning journey.
- Learn about new technologies through exploration and play.

All of the above actions can be more easily achieved these days through the use of social media and new technologies. Your peers and mentors will be an excellent learning resource you can tap into and social media can strengthen these supportive relationships. I explore learning from personal networks in Chapter 8 and from mentors in Chapter 9.

In this chapter I introduce some particular Web 2.0 technologies that you can use to stay on top of new information and trends, keep up with developments in libraries, and also keep up with the emerging technologies themselves. One essential Web 2.0 tool for lifelong learning and for keeping up generally is RSS.

RSS (Really Simple Syndication)

RSS is an information-management tool that helps to solve the problem of information overload. RSS enables you to subscribe to online content and receive notification about newly generated content. Once you subscribe to RSS, you will receive ongoing updates (feeds) from the content provider(s), which may be regular or irregular, depending on how often new content is created. Content may consist of any number of things – news updates, journal alerts, blog posts or any information updates. One way of thinking about RSS is that it is somewhat like having the daily newspaper delivered to your door each day, rather than having to go out and buy it from your local newsagent. This means that instead of visiting your favourite websites to see what new items have been published on your topics of interest, these items are automatically deposited into the online workspace that receives your RSS feed – a separate software application known as the RSS feed reader.

Feed sources are displayed on websites, blogs and the like by a commonly used orange and white icon. Some well known examples of RSS content are news websites such as Yahoo! News at *http://news.yahoo.com/rss/*. Have a look there and elsewhere for the orange and white (or just plain orange) RSS symbol that is the indication that feeds are published frequently from that site.

How does RSS differ from the process of receiving news updates by e-mail? In many ways the two processes are quite similar. However, when you receive updates via e-mail you need to transfer them to a separate folder; they are not so easily retrieved and read. RSS is more efficient and it can be integrated with many other Web 2.0 technologies. The RSS reader software is multifunctional as I will show below. To sum up: receiving e-mail updates is the Web 1.0 way; RSS is the Web 2.0 way.

There are two steps to getting started with the process of subscribing to RSS:

1. Subscribe to an RSS feed reader.
2. Locate RSS feeds and subscribe to them.

The feed reader is the key component of RSS and the place where your feeds will be captured and where you can organise and read them. You should set up the reader first. Have a look at the very simple video introduction to RSS, made by Common Craft: *RSS in Plain English*. The URL is given at the end of the chapter.

RSS feed readers

The RSS feed reader is multifunctional software that displays the RSS feed in a readable style. The most useful feed reader functions include: (1) the ability to set up folders for the feeds; (2) the ability to sort the feeds; and (3) a variety of display options for the feeds.

Google Reader is now the most common RSS feed reader software available: *http://www.google.com/reader*. You need to have established a free Google Account (or Gmail) to sign up for Google Reader. One important advantage of using Google Reader is that if you use other Google products (such as Gmail or Google Groups) you can group them all together and access them using the one Gmail login.

The example of a Google Reader screen in Figure 6.1 shows how the RSS subscriptions have been grouped into subject folders (on the left), while the title list of the retrieved RSS links is displayed on the right, in chronological order. Rather than giving you a step-by-step guide to setting up

Figure 6.1   Google Reader

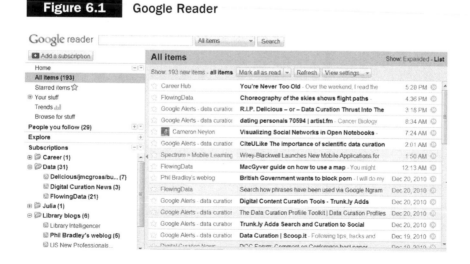

Google Reader, I alert you to some Google Reader video tutorials that will help you get started:

- Google Reader Tutorial: *http://video.google.com/*
- Google Reader in Plain English: *http://www.commoncraft .com/custom-video-google-reader-plain-english*

What other RSS feed readers are there? Unfortunately Bloglines, another popular RSS feed reader, was closed down in 2010. Many web browsers such as Internet Explorer and Mozilla Firefox also handle RSS feeds and display the RSS feeds within the browser's bookmark folders. The web browser approach is a viable option for organising a small number of RSS feeds, but it does not have the full functionality of a dedicated reader such as Google Reader. If you have subscriptions to a large number of feeds (more than a few dozen) it is more efficient to use a purpose-built feed reader. In the section below I describe setting up a start page such as iGoogle and Netvibes, both of which can be used as RSS feed readers. I would suggest that if you have just a few RSS feed subscriptions (say a dozen) then the iGoogle or Netvibes approach could be a suitable way to manage your RSS feeds.

Sources of RSS feeds

Most LIS professionals would understand where to find feeds, because the library's online journal databases and catalogues allow you to set up search topic alerts as a feed, or journal contents page alerts as a feed. Bear in mind that RSS feeds from subscription journal databases may require you to enter a password, whereas feeds available on the open Web normally do not need passwords.

How to subscribe to RSS feeds

There are a number of different RSS logos in use, but as mentioned above the most common is the orange and white RSS logo. To subscribe you need to:

- find the RSS logo on the website offering a feed;
- click on the RSS logo (a screen will appear telling you what to do);
- drag the URL of the feed into your RSS reader, or;
- cut and paste the URL into your RSS reader.

Managing your RSS feeds

The RSS reader software provides an excellent management tool, but you still need to set it up and make a commitment to track your feeds on a regular basis. If you do not efficiently set up and stay on top of RSS, it can become overwhelming and contribute to your overload. This is a personal work and time management issue for you to consider, but it is an important one. Choose your RSS feeds judiciously. My RSS feeds are a combination of blog posts, alerts, newsletters and items of news. I am not averse to deleting any feeds I do not read and adding new ones. Here are some tips for staying on top of RSS:

- Choose feeds to match your current interests.
- Group your feeds in folders.
- Delete any feeds that are no longer relevant.
- Set aside some time each day or week to monitor your feeds.
- Save any important resources into your own information management system, for example on a social bookmarking site (more on this in Chapter 10).

Master RSS and make it part of your overall strategy for becoming a lifelong learner. I will refer to sources of RSS feeds in future chapters.

Start pages

One very effective way to organise your professional updates and arrange the information flow is to set up a 'start page'. This is a personal web page organised by you, using the functionality offered by the start page software. Possible start pages include iGoogle, PageFlakes, My Yahoo! and Netvibes. I will describe two of these: iGoogle and Netvibes. The start page can be made the page where your browser always opens (your homepage). Or, you can bookmark it as a page you frequently visit. I prefer the latter approach because I use my library's homepage as my browser's homepage.

iGoogle start page

I mainly use iGoogle as my start page as it allows me to integrate my other Google products (Google search, Google Groups, Google Analytics, Google Reader, Gmail) into one online workspace. When I open the Google search page, I am taken directly into my iGoogle. (See Figure 6.2.)

iGoogle's ability to operate also as an RSS feed reader makes it particularly useful. The iGoogle RSS reader is less comprehensive than Google Reader, but it is good enough for managing a few RSS feeds. I use this functionality and have created subject tabs to organise my RSS feeds within iGoogle (see Figure 6.2). I usually check for updates and new RSS feeds each day or two. But if I forget, I am taken there

Figure 6.2	iGoogle with RSS feeds

anyway, whenever I conduct a Google search. You can also add useful applications to iGoogle, such as current news, weather, webcams and calendars.

Web widgets and gadgets

These extra iGoogle applications offering news, weather, games and so forth are known as 'web widgets' or 'web gadgets'. iGoogle uses the term gadgets rather than widgets, but they are one and the same. Gadgets are separate web applications that can be embedded into another website. Some examples of library gadgets are catalogue search applications. The rationale behind using library gadgets is they push library content out to all parts of the web. Gadgets can be embedded in blogs, social media sites and third party websites. There are examples of web gadgets on the generic iGoogle start page and you can add some of these to your customised page.

Step by step: setting up iGoogle

If you have a Google Gmail account, setting up an iGoogle start page for current awareness is straightforward (see Figure 6.3). You can feed all or some of your RSS feeds into that page and create various tabs to group your information together. Then, whenever you start up your web browser, the title lines of your RSS feeds will be displayed. There is no need to open each item in the feed, since you can quickly glance down the RSS feed title list to see what is new.

Here is how you set up iGoogle and add RSS feeds:

1. Go to iGoogle *http://www.google.com/ig* and have a look at some of the available content (the gadgets) that you see there. The system suggests some popular content to add to your iGoogle page.

2. Choose some of the available Google-suggested content to add, but don't choose too much because it can be quite distracting if you plan to use this page for your learning space. To retain your selections, you will need to have signed in with your Google Gmail login.

Figure 6.3 iGoogle start page

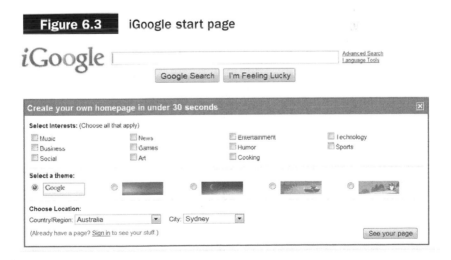

3. Change the look and feel of your page by selecting one of the available themes or artist's background. Rearrange your page by utilising the drag and drop interface, so that the various sections of your page are where you want them to be.

4. Set up RSS feed within your iGoogle page: from your iGoogle page you now add 'stuff'. This takes you to another page and the 'stuff' you add could be an RSS feed or any of the Google gadgets. Copy and paste the RSS feed code into the space provided.

5. Search for some useful library-related gadgets and add them to your page. For example, add the WorldCat catalogue search gadget. After you have finished adding gadgets and RSS feeds, return to your front page (i.e. your iGoogle homepage).

6. Add some extra tabs on your iGoogle page and organize your gadgets and feeds under your tabs. For example, you could have a tab called 'library blogs' and feed all your library blog RSS feeds into this space.

The ability to add and delete tabs enables you to better organise your materials. An iGoogle start page is your private page and is not publicly accessible. iGoogle can also be viewed on a mobile device as can most of the new Web 2.0 tools.

Netvibes

Netvibes is a type of start page or 'dashboard' that can be personalised and shared with others on the web. The company's tagline is 'dashboard everything' and they describe themselves as having 'the first personalized dashboard publishing platform for the Web'. The welcome page is their generic dashboard. When you enter a topic, Netvibes will customise a page (dashboard) for you, incorporating widgets based on your topic. You can choose to accept these widgets into your page or delete them and build your own dashboard from scratch. Netvibes incorporates a Google search box on the main dashboard and provides integration with many Web 2.0 social networking applications. Like iGoogle, the Netvibes page is arranged according to tabs, which you can rearrange on the screen. You can also customise tabs using some pre-arranged themes and colours.

As a lifelong learning tool, Netvibes has the advantage of offering a 'one-stop-shop' page where you can incorporate your other Web 2.0 applications, such as Delicious, LinkedIn, Facebook, Twitter and your RSS feeds. Netvibes can be a private page or a published public page. If you publish your Netvibes page, your RSS feeds can be shared with others on the web. This would be useful for group learning, project work and collaboration.

I have used Netvibes to create a page of RSS feeds I wish to share with a project group. The RSS comprises feeds to blogs, newsletters, social bookmarking tags (covered in Chapter 10), and Yahoo! Pipe feeds (covered below). Figure 6.4 is an example of a Netvibes page: *http://www.netvibes .com/jaygee#Data_management_RSS*

Yahoo! Pipes

Another method for bringing together useful content is to either subscribe to or create your own mashup. Mashups are remixes of web content. However a word of caution – this is for the advanced user. Yahoo! Pipes provides a way of mashing up RSS content. For example, if you find you have a number of RSS feeds and would like to mash them together into one

Figure 6.4 Netvibes, individual page set up with RSS feeds

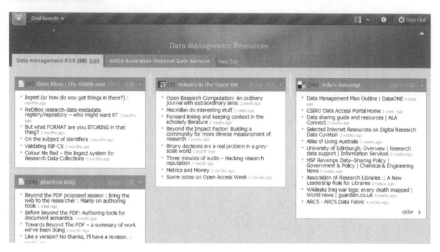

feed, you can do this by building a 'pipe' using Yahoo! Pipes. You will need to have a Yahoo! account to build a pipe. Alternatively you can browse and subscribe to other users' pipes. Yahoo! describes their Yahoo! Pipes service thus:

> Pipes is a free online service that lets you remix popular feed types and create data mashups using a visual editor. You can use Pipes to run your own web projects, or publish and share your own web services without ever having to write a line of code. (*pipes.yahoo.com/pipes/*)

To understand how this works, do a subject search on the Yahoo! Pipes website for pipes that have been created on your subject of interest by other users. If you find some interesting content, you can subscribe within your RSS feed reader, in the manner described above. Many of these pipes have been published and shared on the web for others to access, clone and use. This is real Web 2.0 collaboration at work.

For building your own pipe, you should view the useful online videos on the Yahoo! Pipes website to help you get started. However, I must point out that building your own pipe is more of a stretch for a beginner.

There are three main steps in building your own Yahoo! Pipe:

1. Build your pipe – drag and drop modules onto a canvas and join them together.

2. Describe your pipe – add tags so that others can find your pipe.

3. Publish your pipe – share it on the web.

Published pipes can be found on *pipes.yahoo.com* and may also be picked up by the search engines. Your own pipes will remain private if you choose not to publish them on the web.

Conclusion

> *Education is what remains after one has forgotten everything he learned in school.* (Albert Einstein)

Formal education is just one part of the learning journey. Informal learning is a continual process of personal growth and adapting to change throughout life. Libraries are key institutions that provide lifelong learning opportunities for entire communities. We need to practise what we preach and embrace lifelong learning for career development. There are many ways to do this, but in this chapter I have focused on hands-on learning with Web 2.0 technologies. Learning that contains an element of fun is more likely to be effective and to engage learners at all levels, and Web 2.0 facilitates this engaged approach.

In this chapter I have provided an overview of how career paths are changing and how LIS professionals need to keep learning. In the next chapter I will focus on professional development, providing some specific means for learning with and about Web 2.0 technologies.

References

Bloch, D.P. (2004) The living career: complexity, chaos, connections and career. In G. R. Walz and R. L. Knowdell (eds), *Global realities* (pp. 219–27). Greensboro, NC: CAPS Press.

Hallam, G.C. and McAllister, L.M. (2008) *Self discovery through digital portfolios: a holistic approach to developing new library and information professionals*. Paper presented at the Digital discovery: strategies and solutions: 29th Annual Conference of the International Association of Technological University Libraries (IATUL), Auckland, New Zealand. *http://eprints.qut.edu.au/14048/1/14048 .pdf.*

Longworth, N. and Davies, W.K. (1996) *Lifelong Learning: New Vision, New Implications, New Roles for People, Organizations, Nations and Communities in the 21st century*. London: Kogan Page.

MacLennan, B. (2004) Staying relevant: It's all part of learning. In P. Schontz (Ed.), *The Librarian's Career Guidebook* (pp. 312–24). Lanham, MD: Scarecrow Press.

Maehl, W.H. (2003) Lifelong learning. In J.W. Guthrie (ed.), *Encyclopedia of Education* (2nd edn., Vol. 4, pp. 1480–3). New York: Macmillan Reference USA.

Shumaker, D. (2010) *The embedded librarian* (blog). Retrieved 10 October 2010, from *http://embeddedlibrarian .wordpress.com.*

Webb, J., Gannon-Leary, P. and Bent, M (2007) *Providing effective library services for research*. London: Facet.

Useful weblinks

Common Craft Video. Google Reader in plain English: *http:// www.commoncraft.com/custom-video-google-reader- plain-English*

Common Craft Video. RSS in plain English: *http://www .commoncraft.com/rss_plain_English*

Einstein, Albert (quote): *http://thinkexist.com/quotation/ education_is_what_remains_after_one_has_forgtten/ 15460.html*

Google Reader: *http://www.google.com/reader*

Google Reader Tutorial: *http://video.google.com/*

iGoogle: *http://www.google.com/support/bin/topic.py?topic= 9002*

Netvibes: *http://www.netvibes.com/en*

Yahoo! Pipes: *http://pipes.yahoo.com/pipes/*

YouTube: *http://www.youtube.com*

7

Web 2.0 professional development for your library career

Abstract: This chapter focuses on what the LIS professional can do to take charge of their own professional development and become independent in their learning. It highlights the role of professional organisations in supporting professional development. The chapter provides an overview of how LIS conferences are changing with the use of Web 2.0 technologies – the rise of the conference Twitter backchannel and the spontaneous unconference model. The chapter identifies some sources of online professional development programmes and activities. It describes flexible ways the independent learner can access professional development to advance their career and grow professionally.

Key words: career, Web 2.0, LIS professionals, librarians, professional development, LIS professional associations, library conferences, Twitter, 23 Things, Learning 2.0 Programme, YouTube.

Professional development is one of the *cornerstones* of career advancement for librarians. Maintaining skills and knowledge and developing skills and knowledge in new areas must be a key professional focus at any stage of one's library career. As the Australian Library and Information Association (ALIA) statement on professional development states:

Professional development demonstrates the individual practitioner's personal commitment of time and effort to ensure excellence in performance throughout his or her career. The dynamic and changing library and information environment demands that library and information professionals maintain and continue to develop their knowledge and skills so that they can anticipate and serve the information needs of society and their individual clients. (*http://alia.org.au*)

If you are already in the workforce, professional development may be provided by your employer, but this can be hit and miss, and it may not be targeted at particular library needs or trends. Some other professional development providers in the marketplace are professional associations, independent providers, colleges, universities, library vendors and other commercial organisations. As professionals we need to make an effort to find out what is being offered and participate in formal and informal professional development activities that match our goals.

In Chapter 6, I made the case for becoming an independent learner, dedicated to continuing lifelong learning and I provided some advice on Web 2.0 technologies that could help you stay abreast of new developments in the profession. In this chapter I continue with this theme and focus more specifically on the providers of professional development and the flexible ways in which professional development is now being offered through new technologies.

I outline below some of the sources of library professional development that can be accessed.

LIS professional organisations and professional development

The LIS professional organisations play a strong role in the provision of library professional development. In some countries the professional organisation provides a special status of membership based on a member's continuing professional development activities. For example, in the United Kingdom to achieve chartered librarian membership of the professional body, the Chartered Institute of Library and Information Professionals (CILIP), you need to demonstrate that you have completed a certain amount of professional development. And the Australian Library and Information Association (ALIA) provides the ALIA professional development (PD) scheme which 'is a sub-category of membership which enables ALIA associate and technician members to formally record, and be acknowledged for, their participation in PD activities' (ALIA website, PD). Gaining such credentials is critical for job searchers too.

Professional development activities such as conferences, seminars and workshops are offered by most of the professional organisations and the role of all the LIS professional organisations is strongly behind members' professional development. For example, the UK organisation, CILIP, states:

> Join CILIP and invest in your professional future. Membership provides a range of benefits that help develop your skills and manage your career. Anyone with an interest in information, knowledge or libraries can join. Benefits include:
>
> ■ professional development
> ■ support for your career
> ■ staying informed
> ■ networking and community ... (*http://cilip.org.uk*).

New ways of delivering professional development

Professional development is now being offered differently, thanks to Web 2.0 technologies. Table 7.1 shows how the delivery of professional development has evolved from Web 1.0 to Web 2.0. *What* is covered in professional development and *how* it is delivered have changed. Now we have new elements such as the conference backchannel, flexible delivery modes and mobile access. In Table 7.1 I set out the sorts of changes Web 2.0 is bringing.

Table 7.1 Professional development: Web 1.0 way vs. Web 2.0 way

Professional development (PD) the Web 1.0 way	Professional development (PD) the Web 2.0 way
Conferences	Conferences incorporating wikis, blogging, microblogging, social networking, live chat, SMS, streaming video, online groups, backchannel, mobile access, papers on open access, slide sharing of presentations, conference attendance in remote online mode unconferences
Face-to-face seminars and workshops	Webinars and online workshops, incorporating social networking, live chat, backchannel
Lectures and symposia	Webinars, online workshops, mobile access, remote access any time any place
In-house employer provided PD	Individually initiated PD incorporating different online delivery modes for learning styles and technologies: YouTube, webinars
Library-specific customised PD	PD delivered in online mode, enhanced with social networking
Higher education courses through paid enrolment	Higher education courses through free open courseware

Table 7.1 shows that emerging technologies are enabling a variety of professional development formats such as online webinars, conference backchannels, unconferences, remote access to proceedings and other flexible modes of delivery. I will now expand on some of these developments and the choices they offer for library professionals.

LIS conferences and their career advantages

Conferences are at the core of LIS professional activities. They provide all LIS professionals with golden opportunities to hear from experts in the field, to meet colleagues and engage with the critical issues for the profession. Conferences allow us to set aside time for blue-sky thinking and problem solving. A good conference will include sessions that set out big-picture trends in the global environment, as well as sessions covering experiences from workers at the coalface. Attending a conference can help you make the connections between the external environment and the workplace. Most attendees return from a conference with their batteries recharged, ready for action.

The LIS professional associations provide many of the conferences and they come in various forms. They may be large general library conferences, incorporating the whole span of professional interests, or more specific conferences that target particular library sectors (for example special libraries, school libraries) and particular library groups (for example new graduates).

LIS conferences normally attract several high calibre keynote speakers who are leaders in the profession. Typically, a conference will run over several days and consist of a range of activities including keynote speakers, presentation of papers by experts in the field, break-out sessions, discussion forums, debates, pre-conference workshops and trade exhibitions.

You will benefit from conference attendance on a number of fronts: for lifelong learning, professional development and networking. Some of the larger LIS conferences, such as the American Library Association (ALA), offer mentors and buddies to assist attendees who may be at their first conference. Other conferences have a section for new graduates. Students and early-career attendees may benefit from having a conference mentor, if this is on offer. Similarly, more experienced attendees may make themselves available to mentor the 'newbies'.

Without doubt, conferences are an expensive element of your professional development. There is the initial registration fee; there could also be pre-conference and post-conference workshops, which may involve an additional cost. If you need to travel and stay in a hotel, pay for transport and living expenses, this will add to the outlay. To offset costs, most conferences offer an early-bird registration discount, as well as a discount if you are a member of the sponsoring professional organisation. Check out whether there may be scholarships provided for conference attendance in your area or whether your workplace can subsidise your attendance in return for you bringing the knowledge back.

Getting the most out of conference attendance

In order to get the most value from your conference experience you need to be organised and manage your time. Peruse the conference programme before you arrive and mark off your choice of sessions to attend. Most programmes include a useful abstract for each paper, indicating what the session will cover. Sometimes sessions are cancelled, which may involve rethinking your plan for the day. Do the rounds of the trade and exhibition hall and meet the library vendors and find out about new products.

While at the conference you should endeavour to:

1. Expand your *learning* by:

   - downloading the program ahead of time and checking off all the sessions that you wish to attend, even if they clash;

   - attending sessions on new topics, outside your comfort zone;

   - taking time to speak with library vendors and attending their demonstration sessions.

2. Expand your *networks* by:

   - using your networks to make contact, before you arrive, with colleagues who are attending;

   - checking the delegates list to see who is there;

   - trying not to gather with people you know – chatting to the person next to you, seeking out new people and exchanging business cards.

Post-conference reflection

As soon as possible, while the information is fresh in your mind, write up your impressions or write a conference report. Reflect on what you have learned and how you can apply any new ideas you have encountered. If you are not currently in employment, did you pick up any suggestions on new library areas you can explore? Did you meet new people who could be approached about work? If so make post-conference contact with them, following up with a polite e-mail. On your return from the conference, if there is an opportunity, you should offer to do a presentation on the conference – to focus your thoughts and consolidate the experience.

Conferences in the time of Web 2.0

These days, with the incorporation of Web 2.0 and social networking into the conference format, delegates can have an enhanced conference experience. Many conferences now incorporate new technologies, such as wikis, blogs, podcasts, live chat, streaming video and online community forums. Informally, many participants are using the social networks to establish pre-conference contact with fellow attendees. During the conference the 'backchannel' is playing a new role as a place for multi-layered interactions between delegates and non-delegates (see below). Thanks to new technologies, the contemporary conference can have an impact far beyond the actual event. Speakers often share their presentations on the web (for example on SlideShare). Papers may be placed on open-access repositories, sometimes even before the conference. Live audio and video coverage of the event may be stored for asynchronous access. The official conference blog provides a permanent commentary on the conference highlights and key themes. Some conference delegates write their own useful summary blog posts too.

While at the conference, there are several technologically enriched ways to tune in to the proceedings. Some conferences provide free WiFi, so delegates can access events from anywhere in the venue via their mobile devices: iPads, smart phones and so forth. Another new way to 'attend' a conference is as an online delegate, whereby you participate online, from a remote location. Where the conference is in a similar time zone this can be a good option, if you cannot be there. There is a trend now among Twitter afficionados to follow the conference reports and commentary from delegates' tweets, without actually being present at the conference. See below for some discussion of this phenomenon known as the Twitter backchannel.

Suggested actions for getting the most from social technologies surrounding the conference are:

- read the blog posts before the event to find out local news;
- join the online conference community group or forum, if there is one;
- subscribe to an RSS feed of conference updates;
- if you are on Twitter, establish contact with others before the conference, by using the conference Twitter hash tag when you post a tweet;
- attend the Twitter Tweetup (meeting) at the conference, if there is one.

LIS conferences provide golden opportunities for networking and learning about trends and developments. If you have the opportunity (and funds) to attend a conference in a related area, then do so. In my experience conferences in other disciplines can be relevant and give a different perspective on common issues. For example, in the university sector, conferences on the first-year student experience or on teaching and learning are pertinent. In public libraries, conferences on local history or children's literature may also be relevant.

The conference backchannel

If you have attended a conference within the last few years you will have observed that many delegates are busily tapping away on their laptops, or working on other mobile devices during the presentations. In most cases these delegates will be microblogging using Twitter, an activity that is generating interaction referred to as the 'conference backchannel'. It is another layer of conference communication that some say is the online equivalent to passing notes in class. What role does the backchannel play and does it add value to the conference experience? Many Twitter microbloggers report that Twitter provides them with a medium for taking notes and engaging more deeply with the conference subject matter. A side benefit is that other tweeters can pick up on the Twitter messages and contribute as well.

Microblogging data can be captured and some early textual analysis studies on the backchannel phenomenon are starting to appear in the literature (Ross, Terras, Warwick and Welsh, 2011). Their initial research findings show that the backchannel is a complex space with a myriad of conversations taking place:

> The digital backchannel constitutes a multidirectional complex space in which the users make notes, share resources, hold discussions and ask questions as well as establishing a clear individual online presence. The use of Twitter as a platform for conference backchannels enables the community to expand communication and participation of events amongst its members. (Ross et al., 2011)

The backchannel may play a role in enhancing learning. However, this would be difficult to verify and measure. What we can state is that the backchannel is a collaborative space where conference papers are discussed and some conference goers are engaged in making meaning of new ideas.

Now, some conference presenters are taking participants' questions via the Twitter backchannel and incorporating their responses into the presentations. Time will tell if this will develop as a permanent feature of the modern conference.

Conference bloggers and microbloggers are performing a valuable conference reporting service that reaches an audience far beyond those who are actually physically present. In fact, the conference backchannel output can be seen as providing a professional development service to those who cannot attend. The backchannel data can now be preserved as an archive available for all to peruse.

If you are on Twitter, I recommend that you incorporate 'LIS conference backchannel monitoring' into your informal professional development action plan. The following steps will help you:

- Find out when interesting upcoming LIS conferences are happening.
- Mark the date(s) in your diary.
- Check the conference website to see what Twitter hash tags will be used.
- During the conference follow the Twitter hash tag (conduct a Twitter search for the hash tag to find it).

Ask your colleagues on Twitter to help you with this, if you are unsure how to proceed.

The unconference

Another new mode of professional development is the unconference. In recent years the library unconference has become a feature of LIS professional development in countries such as the United States, United Kingdom, Canada and Australia (Greenhill and Wiebrands, 2008). These events have evolved from the 'bar-camps' started a few years ago, mainly by geeks and followers of new media. The unconference is generally facilitated using the 'open spaces' model, whereby the daily programme is unstructured and session topics are decided on the day. During an unconference, the program is decided upon and events unfold according to the wishes of the participants at the time. Library unconferences tend to be more casual and techie than traditional conferences and often include sessions on emerging technologies and a hands-on component, showcasing new gadgets and devices. What the unconference lacks, in terms of high profile speakers and peer-reviewed papers, is more than made up for by the currency of the presentations, the relaxed atmosphere and the enthusiasm of the participants.

Local unconference events are normally promoted through the online social networks and library electronic discussion lists. Unconferences are mostly organised by groups of volunteers using online collaboration software such as a wiki. They are usually free events and may be sponsored by local libraries, rather than commercial vendors. Undoubtedly the free unconference is a more accessible professional development option for new graduates as well as being a more informal environment for networking.

23 things and the Learning 2.0 Programme

As an independent learner what content should you include in your professional development plan? This will depend on your particular job needs and circumstances. However, learning about the emerging technologies themselves is essential.

The Learning 2.0 Program is an online programme that introduces the beginner to a broad range of Web 2.0 technologies. The programme has become known in the library world as 'the 23 Things' because it contains '23 things' for learners to work through, and each thing is a new Web 2.0 tool. The original programme covers a cross-section of technologies such as blogs, wikis, podcasts, video sharing and social book-marking. Learning 2.0 was developed by Helene Blowers (2006) as an online professional development program for the staff at the Public Library of Charlotte & Mecklenburg County (PLCMC) in North Carolina, USA. Its content has been made freely available under a Creative Commons licence, which means that other libraries can run the programme (giving due acknowledgement) in their own workplaces. In fact, many libraries around the world have offered Learning 2.0 to inform staff about Web 2.0 and its place in libraries. The programme was designed to raise awareness of Web 2.0 and to encourage participants to reflect on their learning and envisage the use of the technologies in the library context.

The beauty of the Learning 2.0 Programme is its flexibility: it can be adapted and updated to accommodate new technologies and different workplace needs, and the delivery mode can be altered. The content of the original 23 activities can still be found on the PLCMC Learning 2.0 Blog: *http:// plcmclearning.blogspot.com/*. Hundreds of libraries worldwide have adapted Learning 2.0 from the original version and the PLCMC Learning 2.0 site provides a list of these libraries and links to many of the worldwide versions of the programme. Some libraries have kept their versions of Learning 2.0 behind a login, however the majority have not, and these sites are freely available on the web.

Accessing the Learning 2.0 Programme as an independent learner

Importantly, you should note that you do not need to be associated with a workplace that offers Learning 2.0 in order to gain access to the content. It is a self-paced, unmediated programme that can be accessed by anyone, anywhere. The content consists of readings and exercises with audio and video centred around a particular technology. Independent learners can either work through the program in a sequence of steps, or pick out a particular technology topic for a refresher. There is no need to complete all 23 activities in any particular sequence because each activity is more or less self contained. All you require is the time and motivation.

It is essential to find a recent version of Learning 2.0 as, being a technology-based program, a few of the original 2006 activities are now somewhat dated. One recent updated example of Learning 2.0 is the 2010 version developed by the University of Cambridge and made available on the 23 Things Cambridge blog (see the Cambridge list of '23 things' below). I strongly suggest accessing this programme and completing the activities, or cherry picking the content for information about the particular technologies of interest. Also, you may wish to check the original PLCMC Learning 2.0 site for other recent versions (see the URL in the reference list). Bear in mind that most versions of the 23 activities are set out as a sequence of blog posts numbered 1-23. This means that if you want to follow the sequence chronologically from the beginning, you need to scroll down and start with to the oldest blog post.

List of 23 things from University of Cambridge Library

As I have mentioned, there are many adaptations of Learning 2.0. What is included in a public library programme may be different from that of an academic library. The University of Cambridge programme includes the following list of 23 things reflecting the typical Web 2.0 learning needs of university library staff in 2010:

1. Set up your Google ID and build an iGoogle page.
2. Add the RSS feed of the Cam23 blog to your iGoogle page.
3. Create your own 23 Things blog on which you will record your progress.
4. Register your blog. Add a screenshot. Explore other Cam23 blogs.
5. Use Doodle to schedule a peer support meeting with another participant.
6. Sign up for Google Calendar and add it to your iGoogle page.
7. Create a Twitter account and interact with other Cam23 'tweeple'.
8. Review your blog tags.
9. Explore Flickr.
10. Use images and Flickr Creative Commons.
11. Explore SlideShare.
12. Investigate Delicious.
13. Reflection week. Think about what you've explored so far and the tools you may adopt.
14. Explore LibraryThing.
15. Create a library or personal LibraryThing account.
16. Explore library Facebook pages.
17. Use LinkedIn.
18. Explore Zotero and Mendeley.
19. Blog about using the Things for library marketing.
20. Create a Google Document and share it.

21. Explore podcasting: YouTube, Audacity and iTunes.

22. Explore and evaluate a selection of wikis.

23. Explore Wordle and blog about your Cam23 experience.
                              (University of Cambridge Library, 2010)

Learning 2.0 encourages learners to actively engage with Web 2.0 technologies and start using them. Learning through play is an inherent philosophy behind the Learning 2.0 programme and the theme runs strongly through the Web 2.0 movement generally. With the proliferation of gadgets and mobile devices you need to take a hands-on approach to finding out how they work.

Devices and gadgets: learning through play

Unless you actually play with some of these new devices you will not begin to conceptualise their impact on libraries. LIS professionals need to adopt a 'learning through play' approach with mobile devices, ebook readers and so forth. It is no surprise that some LIS conferences now include a component of hands-on sessions with new gadgets and devices.

In this rapidly changing area there is a plethora of devices. If you do not already own a few of the devices, I advise you to consider purchasing some of them. Examples of devices you may encounter in your libraries, and will need to know about are:

- iPads
- tablets
- USB flash drives
- many versions of iPods and various other mp3 players

- ebook readers (the Kindle, Kobo, etc.)
- iPhones, Androids, Blackberries and other smart phones.

As the uptake of mobile devices soars, LIS experts are writing about the effect of this on libraries and information professionals. For example, Gerry McKiernan's blog Spectrum is 'devoted to documenting any and all topics relating to mobile learning, mobile library services, and mobile technologies'. (*http://mobile-libraries.blogspot.com/*)

I turn now to some other online sources that you can access for professional development opportunities.

YouTube for professional development

YouTube, the popular Internet source of streaming video, needs no introduction. However, you may not have thought about using YouTube for professional development. Undoubtedly, the YouTube site includes many amateur videos of mediocre quality, but among the dross there are some priceless treasures on all manner of subjects. Use the YouTube search feature to find professional development videos, for example instructional videos on new technologies and videos of seminars and conference presentations. Many universities and professional organisations have their own YouTube channel where you can access free content. Lectures, seminars and even whole courses are available.

Some of the library professional associations have useful content on YouTube, for example:

- CILIP Marketing: *http://www.youtube.com/user/CILIP Marketing*
- AmLibraryAssociation: *http://www.youtube.com/user/ AmLibraryAssociation*

You can subscribe to YouTube channels and get informed when new material is added. There are two YouTube access levels. At the basic level YouTube is a free service and the videos are available on open access. Or you can sign up for a YouTube account. Sign-in access is also free, and provides extra options, such as the ability to:

- upload and share videos;
- comment on, rate, and respond to favourite videos;
- build playlists of favourite videos.

YouTube is owned by Google and can be accessed from the same login screen if you have accounts on both. There are other sites for streaming videos (e.g. Vimeo and Yahoo! Video), but YouTube is the most popular. Regardless of which site you use, endeavour to incorporate online videos into your Web 2.0 toolkit for learning *about* technology and learning *with* technology.

Open education courseware

If you know where to locate it, academic courseware is an excellent source of professional development content in all subject areas. Universities and academies of higher education have traditionally been closed institutions that guard their intellectual property; however, this is changing. There is a worldwide movement in support of open educational resources (OER), whereby course materials, comprising whole courses, units, modules and learning objects are being made freely available on the web. As a result individual learners have access to some high quality course materials from some of the major institutions of higher education. Some examples are Massachusetts Institute of Technology (MIT) and the Open University's OpenLearn, which offers free access to course materials. I have listed the URLs for these two institutions at the end of the chapter.

Webinars

Yet another new way to access professional development is to enrol in a webinar, which is a seminar or course delivered via the web. Webinars are frequently free and may be self-paced or mediated. Unlike the one way transmission model of the webcast, the webinar includes interactive elements – the ability to give, receive and discuss information. Webinars are particularly popular in Web 2.0 and technology areas, and many of those available are library-related.

Webinars are transmitted by various commercial and professional organisations. Library-related webinars are provided by companies such as OCLC, O'Reilly Media, Illuminate, EDUCAUSE, WebJunction (see below) and professional groups such as the Association of College and Research Libraries (ACRL). To locate webinars in your area you could try searching the Web for 'webinars' and 'library' and your region. You will need to be aware of time zone differences if the webinar is being run from outside your region. Members of the North East Florida Library Network (NEFLIN) have produced a convenient list of library-related webinar providers in the United States (see the blog: *http://neflin2.blogspot.com/*).

WebJunction

Based in North America, WebJunction provides online training courses, webinars, events and discussions aimed mainly at public library staff. As their website states:

Since our launch in 2003, the WebJunction has helped more than 50,000 library staff build the job skills they need to meet the challenges of today's libraries ... our focus on library technologies, management, and services, along with public access in small and rural libraries, ensures that public librarians are equipped to meet local needs in their communities. (*http://www .webjunction.org/home*)

WebJunction courses and webinars are reasonably priced and some of their courses are free. Archives of some WebJunction courses (slides, PDFs) are put up on the Web after the event. You can join the WebJunction community, establish a profile and be informed about new courses.

Conclusion

The landscape of LIS professional development is changing. Due to new technologies you can now access a huge variety of conferences, online courses, seminars and webinars. You can access them from your desktop or mobile device, when you like and where you like. You can tune in to the conference backchannel from anywhere in the world to participate in the global online learning community and follow conference activities. Ongoing professional development is essential if you are to move forward in your career, and with new technologies is it much more accessible than in the past.

References

Blowers, H. (2006) *Learning 2.0* (blog). Retrieved 1 March 2007, from *http://plcmclearning.blogspot.com/*.

Greenhill, K. and Wiebrands, C. (2008) *The unconference: a new model for better professional communication.* Paper presented at the Poropitia outside the box: LIANZA Conference, Auckland, New Zealand. *http://opac.lianza .org.nz/cgi-bin/koha/opac-detail.pl?bib=383.*

LIScareer.com. (2000–10) *Career Strategies for Librarians.* Retrieved 21 October 2010, from *http://www.liscareer .com/.*

Ross, C., Terras, M., Warwick, C. and Welsh, A. (2011) Enabled backchannel: Conference Twitter use by digital humanists. *Journal of Documentation, 67(2).*

Useful weblinks

American Library Association. ALA Learning: *http://www .ala.org/ala/onlinelearning/about/index.cfm*

Australian Library and Information Association (ALIA) website: *http://alia.org.au*

Australian Library and Information Association (ALIA). Professional development: *http://www.alia.org.au/policies/ professional.development.html*

Chartered Institute of Library and Information Professionals (CILIP): *http://cilip.org.uk*

NEFLIN. Library webinars (list): *http://neflin2.blogspot.com/*

Massachusetts Institute of Technology (MIT). OpenCourse Ware *http://ocw.mit.edu/index.htm*

McKiernan, G. Spectrum > Mobile learning, libraries, and technologies: *http://mobile-libraries.blogspot.com/*

Open University. OpenLearn: *http://openlearn.open.ac.uk/*

University of Cambridge Library. 23 Things Cambridge blog: *http://23thingscambridge.blogspot.com/*

WebJunction: *http://www.webjunction.org/home*

YouTube: *http://www.youtube.com*

8

Networking for your LIS career

Abstract: This chapter discusses networking, one of the cornerstones of the LIS career. It highlights the crucial role that networks play in professional learning and development. The chapter describes three functions of professional networks: (1) to provide support; (2) to enable professionals to exert influence; and (3) to facilitate professional learning. The chapter explains new learning theories for the digital environment and how these apply to LIS professional development. It describes the personal learning network approach to career learning. The chapter also provides an overview of some Web 2.0 technologies that are useful for developing networks for career advancement and progress.

Key words: career, Web 2.0, LIS professionals, librarians, networking, personal learning networks, PLNs, cloud computing, wikis, Google Groups, Yammer, LinkedIn.

Networking is a central tenet of career development and one of what I call the *three cornerstones* of the LIS career. Librarians need to be good networkers: we live in a networked society and our profession is at the forefront of connecting communities to information and building online networks. But we need to turn this propensity for networking with our clients into building our own professional career networks.

In this chapter I focus on building career networks – face-to-face networks and online networks – using some Web 2.0 tools. This chapter extends the learning and development themes of the two previous chapters: lifelong learning

(Chapter 6) and professional development (Chapter 7). It also reinforces previous chapters: Chapter 4 on marketing and Chapter 3 on social networking sites, and it foreshadows what I cover in Chapter 9 on mentoring.

Why do you need to network?

Networking is vital for sustaining and advancing your career. A network gives you access to a pool of experts who can give you support and advice. Also, and most importantly, a network can form part of your learning and career development. Priscilla Shontz puts it like this:

> Networks provide information, support, development and influence. You develop your network of experts … people you can go to for certain types of information. Some network contacts offer support by offering moral support or practical help. Mentors and experts in your network can help further your professional development and training. Networks can help enhance your influence and visibility, and can open doors for your career. (Shontz, 2002)

Note that Shontz has outlined four main functions of networks: first, networks are for providing information; secondly, networks are for providing support; thirdly, networks are for development; and fourthly, networks are for enabling influence.

I group these into just three types of functions of career networks, which I call:

1. networks of *support* for your career;

2. networks of *influence* for your career;

3. networks of *learning* for your career.

In this chapter I expand on these three vital career network functions and describe the characteristics of each. I then move on to *how* you go about cultivating networks – a critical stage that takes time, persistence and a certain strategy to achieve.

Networks for career support

Supporting networks can provide you with help and advice at any stage in your career journey and on numerous professional matters. For example, as an early-career professional, you can receive support from colleagues or mentors which helps alleviate the anxiety of breaking into a new career. Or a collegial support network could assist you in preparing for a job interview, or give you moral support when the going gets tough. As a mid-career or late-career professional, you may receive support from colleagues or mentors that can help you make important decisions, such as which direction to take in your career, or which course to study for your professional development. The support and encouragement you receive at critical times and on a daily basis can mean the difference between staying put and moving on to greener pastures; between enrolling in further studies and taking on a new position. In fact, at any point of your career, support networks play a pivotal role.

Who could the people in your network be? Those who form your network could be colleagues, professional acquaintances, former teachers, tutors, fellow workers or managers. They may be located within your close circle or, thanks to online social technologies, they could be from the global library community. They may be peers, mentors or experts in the field. Mentors perform a special role in giving personal support (see Chapter 9).

Support networks enable you to:

- tap into a pool of experts;
- solve work-related problems;
- get career advice;
- use networks as a sounding board for new ideas.

Support often results in a mutually beneficial two-way exchange. On Twitter, for example, it is common for members of the network to pose questions and others to respond in a spirit of collegiality. Thus support is given and expertise is shared across the network.

Networks for career influence

Networks help you to build relationships, expand your professional contacts and have influence beyond your immediate circle. For example, if you work in a one-person special library you would need to build a network of influence so that you can communicate your value to the company/organisation. In a larger library you may be able to form a network of work colleagues, comprising professionals from within and without the library. A network enables you to exert influence and, in turn, market yourself and build your brand, in the manner described in Chapter 4.

Networks of influence enable you to:

- meet new people and expand your contacts;
- find out who are the LIS movers and shakers;
- market and build your brand;
- enhance your visibility;
- hunt for jobs.

I turn now to how a learning network can help you build the knowledge and skills that are necessary if you want your career to thrive.

Learning networks and your career

Following on from my discussions of lifelong learning (Chapter 6) and professional development (Chapter 7), this section is concerned with learning networks. Learning through professional networks can add to and enhance your learning independently as a lifelong learner and your professional development. Furthermore, being part of a learning network can boost your career development and job satisfaction.

I discuss learning networks in the next few pages, explaining some of the theories behind networking and learning and networked learning communities. I begin by considering the current research on networks and online learning. Some learning experts and theorists, who are undertaking research about networks and learning, believe that we need a new learning theory to explain learning in the Internet age. For example, Steve Wheeler on his learning technology blog, 'Learning with 'e's', frequently writes about learning networks – what they are and how to develop them: *http://steve-wheeler.blogspot.com*. Research on new learning theories is important for the LIS field as we move into an era of rapid change, where some librarian roles are becoming aligned with the role of the online learning specialist.

Connectivism is one of the new learning theories that attempts to explain how, due to the widespread impact of networked technologies, human learning needs to be re-examined and explained differently. Canadian educator

George Siemens asserts that connectivism is 'a learning theory for the digital age' (2005). Some librarians have picked up on the theory of connectivism, because it promises to help us understand our use of online networks for learning and career development. An elaboration of this theory follows.

Connectivism and learning networks

In essence, connectivism is a learning theory that focuses on human networks and the connections between people as being paramount for learning. Siemens and others state that it is no longer appropriate to theorise about learning as something that occurs just in our heads. The global Internet has caused a fundamental paradigm shift that opens up new connections, and new ways to understand and explain learning, as Siemens explains:

> The pipe is more important than the content within the pipe. Our ability to learn what we need for tomorrow is more important than what we know today ... Connectivism presents a model of learning that acknowledges the tectonic shifts in society where learning is no longer an internal, individualistic activity. (Siemens, 2005)

The 'pipe' that Siemens is talking about is our learning network that connects us to others who are knowledgeable, and who may provide guidance and professional knowledge. I have discussed in previous chapters that it is imperative for professionals to keep learning in the dynamic, changing LIS environment. Establishing a network of colleagues and experts to support ongoing learning is a necessary part of one's career learning and development strategy.

'I store my knowledge in my friends'

Another way of thinking about this is that it is more important to be able to find someone who knows than it is to know the answers oneself. Individually, we cannot know everything and learning happens through our connections with others. According to 'corporate anthropologist', Karen Stephenson:

> Experience has long been considered the best teacher of knowledge. Since we cannot experience everything, other people's experiences, and hence other people, become the surrogate for knowledge. *'I store my knowledge in my friends'* is an axiom for collecting knowledge through collecting people. (Stephenson, 1998)

For library professionals this means that our career learning networks of colleagues and experts are vital to our lifelong learning and professional development. In practical terms, your network can be where you go to get specific information, find out how to implement a new technology, or 'phone a friend' for help. As discussed above, Shontz states that as an LIS professional you need to 'develop your network of experts ... people you can go to for certain types of information' (2002). One example of such a network of experts is the concept known as the personal learning network or PLN, which I will now explain.

Personal learning networks (PLNs)

Having a PLN can provide you with an entrée into a wider group of knowledgeable colleagues. But what are PLNs and how are they formed? PLNs evolved within the discipline of education. Teachers, school librarians, instructors and educational technologists are keen users of PLNs. But the idea is catching on among librarians too. Taking the lead from educators, librarians are now looking at establishing PLNs (Bennett and Wiebrands, 2010). A PLN can be defined as 'a group of people who can guide your learning, point you to learning opportunities, answer your questions, and give you the benefit of their knowledge and experience' (Tolbin as cited by Bennett and Wiebrands, 2010). PLNs can also provide support and influence, but their *raison d'être* is to enable development and learning.

Learning networks, such as PLNs, enable you to:

- learn in a collaborative environment;
- get moral support from colleagues;
- get answers to your questions;
- share your problems;
- share your experiences and achievements.

Your PLN can be a network of affinity, such as with fellow workers and colleagues. It can also be a network of proximity, that is, with people in close geographical range. And it may include people you have met face-to-face or those you have met online. As I discussed in Chapters 2 and 3, social networks can snowball, as friends introduce you to their friends, in an ever expanding circle.

Thus learning networks are formed in a variety of ways and can range from being ad hoc to being strategic. You can establish your own PLN by becoming an active participant on a social network, such as Twitter or LinkedIn, and by selectively adding key people into your network in ways that have been described previously (in Chapters 3 and 4). Alternatively, a mentor can assist you to expand your network. Once you have started connecting with people in your network, you can start to use many of the Web 2.0 social technologies to maximise contact and exposure. Useful technologies for this are blogs, wikis, Facebook, LinkedIn and Twitter. Sue Waters' blog (2009) on learning with Web 2.0 includes many posts on PLNs and on the technologies you can use to set one up. I expand on some of them in the paragraphs below.

How do you cultivate a network?

Developing a network is like establishing a garden: it needs your careful attention and cultivation. The more time and effort you put into building up your network, the greater will be the rewards. Networks expand over time, and may eventually contract. But they all need to be sustained and nourished. You may have several networks, such as a network of face-to-face colleagues and an online social learning network. Networks take time, patience and persistence to get going.

Tips for cultivating networks:

- Join a professional organisation and actively engage with colleagues.
- Join a special interest group, if there is one in your area.
- Volunteer to go on a committee.
- Help to plan a conference or run an event yourself.
- Join a non-library committee in your workplace.
- Take the long-term view and be persistent.

You may not always have the chance to meet colleagues and network face-to-face. In some work areas there are more opportunities for this than in others. Many librarians work in small libraries and may be isolated from collegial support. With online social networks, there are now many more opportunities to network online. Having an online and a face-to-face connection can strengthen your links with other professionals.

Cloud computing

Before I cover some specific Web 2.0 technologies for networking, I will elaborate on the term 'cloud computing', since it is a term you will come across in the context of Web 2.0. Many of the Web 2.0 tools I have discussed in this and other chapters reside 'in the cloud' (a metaphor for the Internet):

> Cloud computing is web-based processing, whereby shared resources, software, and information are provided to computers and other devices on demand ... it is a by-product and consequence of the ease-of-access to remote computing sites provided by the Internet. This frequently takes the form of web-based tools or applications that users can access and use through a web browser as if it were a program installed locally on their own computer. (Wikipedia, Cloud computing)

The web-based tools or applications referred to above can range from enormous datasets to individual documents or web tools. Many of the Web 2.0 tools that are used for social networking are cloud-based. For example, blogging tools such as Blogger, wiki tools such as PBWiki or Wetpaint Wiki, and web-based e-mail tools such as Gmail or Yahoo! Mail are cloud-based applications. They reside in the cloud (on the Internet) and not on your own workstation or local network. Some examples of Web 2.0 tools that are *not* cloud-based are locally hosted wiki and blog tools.

In earlier chapters I discussed the participative nature of Web 2.0 and hence of networking. Most of the Web 2.0 tools I have referred to in the book thus far are used for networking in some way. However, for convenience I have spread different Web 2.0 tools throughout the chapters and pin-pointed the career application for each tool.

Wikis for networking

When you start to build a network of colleagues and peers, one key Web 2.0 tool you can use is a wiki, particularly if you are engaged in a group project. A wiki is a 'collaborative website and authoring tool that allows users to easily add, remove and edit content' (Blowers, 2006). Wikipedia is the best-known wiki and an excellent example of Web 2.0 collaboration, having been built through the combined efforts of the worldwide Wikipedia community. Wikis are typical examples of the collaborative nature of Web 2.0: any member of the wiki community can add, edit and (sometimes) delete content. If required, the wiki owner can limit edit/delete permissions to certain individuals.

Librarians have been quick to adopt the wiki approach to many practices, such as group networking and conference planning. You may be invited to join and contribute to a wiki. Participating in wiki collaborations can enhance your personal learning development, and benefit the wiki community.

Some examples of collaborative library wikis offering career-relevant information are:

- A Day in the Life of a Library project. A site where librarians post 'day in the life' stories twice a year. (*http://librarydayinthelife.pbworks.com/*)

- Library Success: A Best Practices Wiki. This showcases innovations and success stories from librarians around the world. (*http://www.libsuccess.org/index.php?title=Main_Page*)

There are many choices of software to use if you would like to start your own wiki. Some sites offer a free wiki service, others are free but include some advertising, and others will charge a small fee to provide a wiki without the advertisements. I have used the common wiki softwares of PBWiki and Wetpaint Wiki and find that both provide good functionality. If you wish to start a small career collaboration using a wiki software, there are a number to choose from. The Mashable social networking site has a list, rating many of the current wiki softwares: *http://mashable.com/2008/07/29/wiki-solutions/*.

Google Groups for networking

Google Groups is a popular Web 2.0 tool for career networking and collaborating with colleagues who may be spread across disparate areas (see Figure 8.1). Your Google Gmail login also gives you access to Google Groups. If you have a Gmail account, you can start your own group and invite others in. Or, you may be asked to join a group started by others. The Google Groups website states that Google Groups is 'about helping users connect with people, access information, and communicate effectively over e-mail and on the web' (Google Groups).

A Google group can be formed around any topic and there are several customisable features to enhance the look and

Figure 8.1 Google Groups sign in page

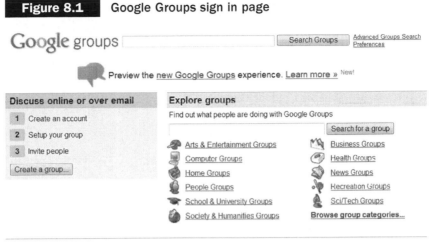

feel of the page. Any sort of networking and groupwork can be done on Google Groups, including large group project work, where participants are spread across various locations. The following are some examples of groups I am involved in, using Google Groups:

- conference planning group
- project planning group
- postgraduate student group
- new technologies group.

Shared discussions on my various Google Groups can cover any topic discussion a group member may start, but some examples are:

- discussing a project plan, new product or idea;
- reading messages and responding publicly, so all in the group can see;
- sharing links to useful information and documents.

Because Google Groups resides in the cloud it does not take up local server space and is not dependent on group members having any special software on their own machines. Only members of the group can view group discussions.

Yammer for networking

Yammer is not as well known a social networking site as Twitter, but it is quite similar in that you can post brief 'micro' blog posts on it. It is an example of what is referred to as 'enterprise social networking' software and as such can enhance your work-based networks and your career. Usually, your place of work will be the instigator for setting up a Yammer account. Yammer can be integrated into Twitter, which means that if you post one message in Twitter and tag it with #yam your message will appear simultaneously on Twitter and Yammer. To enable this function, you need to go into your Twitter settings and link your Yammer account to Twitter. If it is part of your workplace's social media presence, you would be wise to participate in Yammer.

LinkedIn for networking

In Chapters 3 and 4 I discussed the social networking site, LinkedIn. Breeding (2009), Kawasaki (2007) and others have found LinkedIn to be most useful for establishing professional networks of influence for your career. As I stated elsewhere, setting up a LinkedIn profile is an excellent starting point for developing your brand and marketing yourself. LinkedIn is also a helpful career networking tool.

LinkedIn includes the facility for setting up a group within the larger LinkedIn site. The network has a mixture of closed and open groups. As a LinkedIn member, you can search for library groups in your area and join them. Some of the LinkedIn LIS groups are:

- LinkedIn American Library Association (ALA) Group page;
- LinkedIn LIS Career Options Group page (subgroup of LinkedIn ALA);
- LinkedIn CILIP: the Chartered Institute of Library and Information Professionals Group page;
- LinkedIn Internet Librarian International.

You do not need to be an association member to join some of the LinkedIn groups linked to LIS professional associations. For example, the LIS Career Options subgroup's welcome page states:

> If you're not yet a member of the group but would like to be, simply go to the LinkedIn ALA Group page, sign up to be a member of their group (you don't need to be a member of ALA to do this, but sometimes it does take a couple of days before they have a chance to approve your application). Once you've been approved by ALA, go to the LinkedIn ALA Group page, click on the 'More' tab, and then Subgroups. This will bring up the LIS Career Options subgroup, and you can just join from there. (LinkedIn LIS Career Options Group)

The active LinkedIn LIS Career Options group is worth joining. Professionals in this group willingly share their experiences and provide advice and tips to others in the group. Over the time I have been a member, there have been more than fifty career discussions among members on topics ranging from job hunting tips to advice on making a career change. Kim Dority, the group's manager, has linked all the LIS Career discussions into her blog, Infonista (Dority,

2010). It is an excellent place to connect with other professionals and share common interests and problems.

In many ways the LIS groups on LinkedIn play a similar role to the traditional library listservs or e-mail discussion lists. But listservs and elists are the Web 1.0 way, whereas LinkedIn groups are Web 2.0, having all the functionality you would expect from a Web 2.0 tool – profiles, networking and cross-links to other social tools, as I explained in Chapters 3 and 4.

Conclusion

Your professional networks are crucial for exerting influence, receiving and giving support, and developing your career. In his book on characteristics of the twenty-first-century information professional (2006) Dennie Heye rates *networking* as a key characteristic that the LIS professional should acquire.

In Chapter 4 I discussed social media and the four Cs of marketing: content, context, connections and conversations. Networking is very much about the *connections* and *conversations*. In this chapter I have introduced the concept of the personal learning network or PLN that will help in making the connections and starting the conversations. I have also highlighted some more Web 2.0 technologies for networking. It will take time and persistence to develop your networks, but building on the approach of this and previous chapters will put you in a winning position.

References

Bennett, T. and Wiebrands, C. (2010) *Out on the edge: using a personal learning network for continuing professional development.* Paper presented at the ALIA Access 2010, Brisbane, Australia. *http://conferences.alia.org.au/access 2010/pdf/Paper_Thu_1410_Teresa_Bennett.pdf.*

Blowers, H. (2006) *Learning 2.0* (blog). Retrieved 1st March 2007, from *http://plcmclearning.blogspot .com/.*

Breeding, M. (2009) Social networking strategies for professionals. *Computers in Libraries,* 29(9), 29–31.

Dority, K.G. (2010) *Infonista: on being an information entrepreneur.* Retrieved 1 September 2010, from *http:// infonista.com/2010/discussions-list-linkedin-lis-career-options-group/.*

Heye, D. (2006) *Characteristics of the Successful Twenty-first-century Information Professional.* Oxford: Chandos.

Hurst-Wahl, J. (2010) *eNetworking 101: Helping you build & extend your network with social networking tools* (blog). Retrieved 2 November 2010, from *http:// enetworking101.blogspot.com/.*

Kawasaki, G. (2007) *Ten ways to use LinkedIn.* Retrieved 4 August 2010, from *http://blog.guykawasaki.com/2007/ 01/ten_ways_to_use.html#axzz0tSSsFG9b.*

LIScareer.com. (2000–10) *Career Strategies for Librarians.* Retrieved 21 October 2010, from *http://www.liscareer .com/.*

Shontz, P. (2002) *Why Network?* Retrieved 2 November 2010, from *http://www.liscareer.com/shontz_networking .htm.*

Shontz, P. (ed.) (2004) *The Librarian's Career Guidebook.* Lanham, MD: Scarecrow Press.

Siemens, G. (2005) *Connectivism: A learning theory for the digital age. International Journal of Instructional Technology and Distance Learning,* 2(1). Retrieved 2 November 2010, from *http://www.itdl.org/Journal/Jan_05/article01 .htm.*

Stephenson, K. (1998) *What knowledge tears apart, networks make whole. Internal Communication Focus no. 36.* Retrieved 2 November 2010 from *http://www .netform.com/html/icf.pdf.*

Waters, S. (2009) *Baiting the digital hook to build a professional learning community.* Retrieved 2 November 2010, from *http://suewaters.com/2009/06/21/baiting-the-digital-hook-to-build-a-professional-learning-community/.*

Wheeler, S. (2010) *I store my knowledge with my friends. Learning with 'e's.* Retrieved 1 November 2010, from *http://steve-wheeler.blogspot.com/2010/10/i-store-my-knowledge-with-my-friends.html.*

Useful weblinks

Wikipedia. Cloud computing: *http://en.wikipedia.org/wiki/Cloud_computing*

A Day in the Life of a Library project: *http://librarydayinthe life.pbworks.com/*

Google Groups: *https://groups.google.com/*

LinkedIn home: *http://www.linkedin.com/nhome/*

Mashable (blog): Wiki solutions. *http://mashable.com/2008/07/29/wiki-solutions/*

Twitter home: *http://twitter.com/*

Wikipedia home: *http://en.wikipedia.org/*

9

E-mentoring for career development

Abstract: This chapter discusses the role of mentoring in the LIS career and why mentoring is important. It provides an overview of how mentoring can benefit all librarians, especially the early-career librarian. The chapter discusses the new area of e-mentoring and describes some of the Web 2.0 technologies that can be used to facilitate an e-mentoring relationship. It focuses on informal e-mentoring, how to find a mentor online and strategies for initiating a mentoring relationship. The chapter also describes the characteristics of a successful mentoring relationship and provides some case-study examples of mentoring at work.

Key words: career, Web 2.0, LIS professionals, librarians, early career librarians, mentoring, e-mentoring, networking.

As you know, libraries operate within a rapidly changing environment that is heavily influenced by new technologies. Therefore, the library professional's career is a learning journey with continual change and adaptation. Try to find a mentor who can be your guide and coach along your career path. Such a person could provide you with help and advice and an introduction to collegial networks. Mentoring is a tried and true means to support career development that works best when it is an ongoing, mutually beneficial relationship. E-mentoring, using new technology as the mode of communication is becoming the common way of doing mentoring now. E-mentoring relationships can be initiated and sustained using Web 2.0 technologies, such as social networking.

In this chapter I focus on mentoring and Web 2.0 tools for building e-mentoring relationships for your career. The chapter builds on the learning, development and networking themes of previous chapters: lifelong learning (Chapter 6) professional development (Chapter 7) and networking (Chapter 8). During my career I have had the privilege of experiencing positive mentoring relationships from both sides – as mentor and mentee. Throughout this chapter I will refer to my own experience of mentoring and illustrate how I have sustained mentoring relationships using Web 2.0 and other communication technologies.

What is mentoring?

The mentoring story has a long tradition in the West and the word 'mentor' can be traced back to Greek mythology. In Homer's *Odyssey*, Mentor was the teacher, guide and father figure who stayed behind on the island of Ithaca to mind King Odysseus's son while the king went to war. In the past few decades mentoring has been resurrected in various contexts such as in industry, the education sector, and in libraries. Modern day mentoring can be summarised as a relationship where there is mutual need, mutual choice, and trust (Carter and Caldwell, 1993). There are several factors that need to be in place for a relationship to be considered mentoring and characteristics of the relationship are that it is:

1. a two-way, learning relationship that draws upon the knowledge and wisdom of suitably experienced practitioners;

2. designed to fulfil the two broad purposes of career and psychosocial development, with the specific goals of the

relationship being determined by the individuals involved;

3. a relationship developed over time, that is, there is more than just a short-term or passing interest on the part of the mentor and mentee, and the relationship passes through a series of developmental stages. (Ritchie and Genoni, 1999)

Mentoring can be seen as an extension of both networking and professional development, and mentoring programmes are often accessed through the professional organisations, as I outline below. It can bring both personal benefits, contributing to an individual's well-being, and organisational benefits of having well-adjusted employees in the workplace.

What does a mentor do?

A mentor can prompt you to reflect on your existing job and future work aspirations, helping you to answer the hard questions: 'Where is my career going? Which new skills should I be developing? Which part of my job do I want to build on?' (Nankivell and Shoolbred, 1997). Mentors can work with you individually over a length of time and provide you with more focused, in-depth advice than would otherwise be available from a more transient career relationship, such as a networking relationship. In their survey of over 300 LIS professionals, Nankivell and Shoolbred found that these librarians perceived the role(s) of the mentor as:

■ advisor

■ guide

■ support

- coach
- role model
- teacher/tutor
- counsellor
- confidante. (Nankivell and Shoolbred, 1997)

All these roles link strongly to career development and confirm the importance of mentoring at every stage of a library career.

Benefits of mentoring in the workplace

The benefits of mentoring are similar to those of professional development and networking: access to personal development, growth opportunities and learning. Traditionally, in many large organisations an experienced worker was assigned to the new recruit to help him/her learn the ropes. This may no longer be the case and new graduates may be left to fend for themselves. Carter and Caldwell (1993) argue that in the age of organisational downsizing, when some middle management levels have been eliminated, it is more critical to look afresh at mentoring in the workplace. Even where there is a workplace induction programme, new librarians can benefit from mentoring, especially if receiving mentoring from an expert outside the workplace, who brings a different perspective. Many librarians work alone, particularly those in special libraries where there may be few experienced colleagues to call upon for advice. Mentoring is an ideal support mechanism in such cases. But career mentoring opportunities are also provided outside the workplace by professional associations.

Formal mentoring

Many of the LIS professional associations offer formal, structured mentoring programs and links to available mentors and mentoring advice. Librarians working in larger organisations may also be able to access formal mentoring programmes in the workplace, but this is less common. Library professional associations across various English-speaking countries offer a range of options, some of which are listed below:

- The ALA has a mentoring program: New Members Round Table (NMRT): *http://www.ala.org/ala/mgrps/rts/nmrt/ oversightgroups/comm/mentor/mentoringcommittee.cfm*

- The Australian Library and Information Association (ALIA) recognises the importance of mentoring and provides several formal ALIA mentoring schemes that are listed on their website: *http://www.alia.org.au/education/ pd/scheme/*

- The Canadian Library Association has a list of resources, books, journal articles and websites dealing with mentoring, both within and outside the library world: *http://www.cla.ca/AM/Template.cfm?Section=Mentoring*

- CILIP provides a mentor scheme: *http://www.cilip.org.uk/ jobs-careers/qualifications/cilip-qualifications/mentor-scheme/Pages/default.aspx*

- LIANZA has a Mentoring Manual: *http://www.lianza.org .nz/resources/professional-registration/mentoring/lianza-mentoring-manual*

Typically, formal mentoring programmes are set up to serve a specific purpose such as guiding a new career librarian through the acclimatisation process of their first few years in the workforce. Such schemes tend to be hierarchical, whereby an experienced librarian is paired with a new graduate and they may be restricted to new graduates for a fixed time period, rather than available to the profession at large. However, new mentoring models are emerging. Murphy (2008) points out that the mentoring models in organisational psychology and management are more holistic and she advocates that libraries adopt a developmental rather than a hierarchical approach to mentoring relationships:

> library colleagues at all levels of experience and responsibility need to learn together and note the value of seeking out multiple developmental relationships to enhance professional competencies and skills for the future. (Murphy, 2008)

Developmental models of mentoring fit the current reality of workplaces, where career paths are more varied and less well defined. In this broader understanding of the relationship, the mentor can learn from the mentee in a form of reverse mentoring. An example would be a Millennial who has skills in emerging technologies that can be passed on to the more experienced mentor, thus ensuring a quid pro quo arrangement.

Informal mentoring

Informal mentoring allows for more flexibility and there is a greater likelihood of a mutually beneficial relationship developing. However, for an informal mentoring relationship to work, it needs to have some structure. Ideally both parties agree on goals and ground rules before embarking on the venture, otherwise it risks foundering. In informal mentoring participants negotiate the agenda and articulate their objectives and career plans. They decide, if they can, how long the relationship should last and how they will stay in touch. The prompts below may be useful for clarifying goals for such an informal mentoring relationship.

Question prompts for the prospective mentee:

- What are my career objectives?
- What advice do I need from my mentor?
- What skills do I need to acquire?
- How long do I want the relationship to last?
- How will I communicate with my mentor and how often?

Question prompts for the prospective mentor:

- How much time can I commit to the relationship?
- What is my motivation for becoming a mentor?
- How will I communicate with my mentee and how often?
- What networks can I access to help my mentee?
- Do my skills and knowledge match my mentee's needs?
- How can the relationship be mutually beneficial?

When starting out on informal mentoring, it is important for the mentee and mentor to agree on goals and plans, and establish what each party hopes to achieve. In that way, the arrangement stands more chance of being satisfactory for both parties. In practical terms some operational matters should be adhered to: meet deadlines where possible, and commit sufficient time to the relationship.

E-mentoring

In this world of global online communities it is not surprising that mentoring relationships can be formed and sustained via electronic communication technologies. E-mentoring relationships may be pre-existing relationships that continue to thrive online, or they may be relationships that are initiated online using online networks. E-mentoring is defined by Muller as 'a mentoring relationship which uses the tools of electronic communication either to extend or enhance an existing mentoring relationship, or to create one where it would not otherwise exist' (2009).

Many Web 2.0 tools can be used for e-mentoring, for example:

- social networking tools: Facebook, Twitter, LinkedIn;
- content sharing tools: YouTube, Flickr, SlideShare (sharing presentations);
- collaboration tools: wikis, Doodle (meeting set-up), Google Docs (sharing documents, such as resumés);
- professional development tools: Delicious or Diigo (sharing bookmarks), Netvibes (sharing your RSS feeds).

I describe below how I have used Web 2.0 in several e-mentoring relationships, some of which involved e-mentoring with librarians in developing countries. In most cases we had already established a professional connection and used electronic means to provide advice and to stay in touch.

It is possible for an e-mentoring relationship to be formed and sustained totally online, without the participants ever meeting face-to-face, in much the same way as external students take online courses and are tutored and taught online and never actually meet their tutors. I now expand on some of the communication technologies that can be used for e-mentoring.

Table 9.1   My e-mentoring story (1)

A few years ago, I became the mentor for a librarian in a developing country. We already had established a face-to-face professional relationship through some formal institutional linkages. Over time, the relationship evolved into an informal e-mentoring relationship.

In the beginning we established guidelines on what the formal relationship would achieve. The original timeframe for that was two years. Later, when the informal mentoring developed, we adopted a more open-ended time frame.

I provided advice to my mentee on library operational issues, professional development and training and career development. After the more formal arrangement concluded, the relationship developed into more of a career guidance role on my part. I have assisted my mentee with sponsorship and scholarship applications and provided advice on opportunities for undertaking further studies. We have also collaborated in an academic research project.

Over several years we have used e-mail to stay in touch, but have also met face-to-face where the opportunity arose at conferences and so forth. We share professional content using Google Docs for developing research outlines. We also use Facebook and LinkedIn to stay in touch. I would say that while the Web 2.0 technologies were not essential, they have certainly helped to sustain the relationship, which has changed and evolved over time. I find that the use of social networking (particularly Facebook) in developing countries is quite high and it helps to maintain contact.

E-mail for e-mentoring

Even though e-mail is now considered 'old hat', it remains the obvious communication technology of choice for fostering and developing an e-mentoring relationship. It will certainly never replace face-to-face communication, but in many instances personal contact between mentor and mentee is not possible. And even where a face-to-face formal or informal mentoring relationship exists, e-mail exchanges can complement the existing relationship and open up new lines of enquiry. E-mail messages can be more considered than some of the social networking messages, such as those on Twitter, while the simplicity and brevity of social networking messages have distinct advantages, as I will explain later. An e-mail exchange provides a substantial written record that can be accessed later and may prompt new questions and ideas between mentor and mentee. E-mail messages between the two parties remain private, thus ensuring confidentiality is maintained. And e-mail can break down communication barriers arising from status and gender difference and from other factors.

Advantages of e-mail for mentoring:

- It allows for asynchronous communication.

- It suits those corresponding across different time-zones.

- It allows the senders to reflect and consider their words.

- It provides a record of the communication, questions and advice.

- It helps to maintain confidentiality.

- It levels the playing field between parties.

In many cases there may not be the time or opportunity to schedule a face-to-face meeting, so then e-mail becomes an essential tool.

Disadvantages of e-mail for mentoring:

- It does not equal face-to-face communication.

- It can be more time consuming than verbal communication.

There are other communication tools, including Web 2.0 tools for e-mentoring, that have been covered in this and previous chapters, but the critical point in establishing an e-mentoring relationship is to locate a mentor.

Finding a mentor

With the advent of e-mentoring, new possibilities for establishing and sustaining mentoring relationships have opened up. Where would you find a mentor and how do you initiate that relationship?

Finding a mentor takes time and persistence, even when working through your existing networks. Nankivell and Shoolbred suggest that it is 'an active process of assessing potential mentors at every possible occasion' (1997). You could start by approaching the professional bodies, groups and committees you belong to or by putting a call out through library discussion groups, new graduate groups and e-lists. A suitable mentor may be someone with whom you already have a face-to-face relationship, but you may need to go further afield. You will find that social networking sites offer mentoring opportunities, giving you connections with colleagues who have mutual interests. Try posting a message on your existing networks, for example on a LinkedIn library group, if are you a member, or on other online networks Think laterally as to where you may encounter a group of skilled and experienced library professionals. I mentioned in Chapter 8 how social networking sites such as Twitter can be used to develop Personal Learning Networks (PLNs). A mentor may be sought through your PLN, if you have one. It is not inconceivable that you could put feelers out on Twitter to find a mentor, addressing those individuals with whom you already have an established online relationship.

I established a mentoring relationship which initially came about through a group of professional contacts (a PLN) on Twitter. What happened in this case is described in the case study below.

Table 9.2	My e-mentoring story (2)

A new graduate and colleague put out a call for a mentor via a PLN on Twitter and I responded. In this case we already had an existing face-to-face professional relationship, but were working in different cities.

We agreed in general terms to the objectives of the mentoring arrangement, the type of issues needing my guidance and attention, how much time we could devote to the relationship and how often we would communicate.

We continued to communicate via e-mail (mainly), but also on Twitter, Facebook and LinkedIn (using some of the library groups on LinkedIn). We established a Skype connection to talk face-to-face for more complicated and involved discussions.

The types of issues we discussed were: career direction, finding employment, moving between different types of libraries, embarking on further studies, conference attendance and writing for the profession.

Twitter levels the playing field and makes professionals more accessible. Whereas in the past people may have felt reluctant to approach someone online to become their mentor, now this is less likely to be the case. If you have already built up a relationship with a knowledgeable professional on Twitter or other social networks, you could certainly approach him/her to be your mentor, even if you have not met in person.

Characteristics of a successful e-mentoring relationship

Both parties need to have an understanding of what constitutes successful mentoring and work towards developing such a relationship. All mentoring relationships, whether the mode of communication is electronic or not, are built on trust and mutual respect between the partners. Mentor and mentee must agree that their communications, when necessary, remain confidential. The mentee should feel he/she can raise difficult problems and the mentor should be candid and give honest feedback.

Although Kem (2005) and others (Nankivell and Shoolbred 1997; Carter and Caldwell, 1993) report that almost all librarian mentoring experiences are positive, problems can arise. One potential risk is if the mentor is the mentee's immediate line manager. There are existing power structures within all organisations and the mentee could be vulnerable if his mentor was also his manager. Ideally, the two parties should work in different workplaces. An honest and open dialogue between mentor and mentee is more likely if participants are not work colleagues; the mentee can be free to raise difficult issues and the mentor brings an outsider's perspective.

Brockbank and McGill claim the following to be good mentor attributes:

- active listener
- able to observe and reflect back
- empathiser
- prepared to give information
- questioner
- willing to challenge
- able to feed back and summarise. (1998)

All of these characteristics apply equally to both parties in an e-mentoring relationship. The mentor should communicate regularly and be prepared to give feedback and the mentee should ask questions so that the mentor has a starting point for their dialogue. The mentee should be prepared to accept the mentor's advice or criticism.

The lack of time each party is able, or prepared, to devote to the relationship can pose problems. Even in an e-mentoring situation, there may be lack of time to compose a considered response to an e-mail. For this reason using some of the quick, efficient social technologies to stay in touch is ideal. It may be helpful to set a notional time frame to the relationship, so that if time is a factor the mentor knows their commitment has an end date.

Since the mode of communication is the principal point of difference between e-mentoring and mentoring generally, partners in an e-mentoring relationship should decide in the beginning how they will communicate. Communication choices will naturally depend on the nature of particular discussions. E-mentoring communication falls into two categories: (1) private/confidential and (2) public.

- Examples of technologies used for private/confidential e-mentoring communication would be e-mail, Facebook direct message and Twitter direct message.
- Examples of technologies used for public communication would be the Facebook wall and Twitter.

Communication should be reasonably frequent. One of the advantages of using social networking technologies (Facebook, chat, Twitter) in e-mentoring is that the connection can be readily maintained by a quick message. Although most social networking communications are not set up to be private, they mostly have a private messaging facility and this could be used for quick updates. My point here is that where both parties are active users of social networking, their paths will cross and they are more likely to stay in touch.

Thinking outside the box, peer mentoring and non-library mentors

In large organisations, librarians can become isolated. However roles have converged, we now share common ground with other professionals. For example, in a university, academic librarians may be aligned to instructional designers, teachers, researchers and technologists. Therefore, it is entirely possible to find mentors within other disciplines. In my case, I sought a mentor from another department in the university to help me build my knowledge of learning technologies and to advance my career goals.

Table 9.3   Being mentored: my story

While undertaking postgraduate studies in education, I sought out a mentor whose name had been recommended to me by my lecturer. My mentor had skills in project management and in developing web-based services. She was also keen to learn from me what the library was doing to promote and implement Web 2.0 technologies.

Fortunately, we worked on the same campus and agreed to meet fortnightly for face-to-face one hour lunchtime meetings. We decided at the outset that the mentoring relationship would have the specific time span of one year.

Outside the meetings our communication was via phone or e-mail, but later we used Facebook to share brief messages and to chat online.

The topics my mentor advised me on were wide-ranging and included: the application of new learning technologies, the library's Web 2.0 professional development programme and staff development across the organisation. A year later we collaborated again as partners on a major project extending across several institutions.

In this case the mentoring relationship had a specific time span, as each of us later moved into different areas. However, we still maintain an informal, collegial relationship and intend to collaborate again in the future.

That relationship had value as a developmental two-way mentoring relationship. It provided a pathway for me to reach outside the library and extend my organisational networks, to acquire new knowledge and skills from my mentor, and to pass on to my mentor my librarian expertise and knowledge.

Online networks for mentoring contacts

I draw the chapter to a conclusion by mentioning some online networks that, in addition to the LinkedIn groups already covered in previous chapters, provide another source of information about the LIS profession in action.

A Day in the Life of a Library project is a wiki started in 2008 by Bobbi Newman. Twice a year librarians around the world share their stories on the Day in the Life of a Library wiki, describing what they did in their jobs on that day. While strictly speaking it is not a mentoring site, this wiki, and the associated blog posts and links, provide an insight into librarians' working lives. For LIS students or early career professionals it is fascinating to read from the posts how different and varied librarian jobs are (*http://libraryday inthelife.pbworks.com/*).

LISNPN (LIS New Professionals Network) is a network for New Professionals in the Library and Information sector in the UK (*http://www.lisnpn.spruz.com/*).

Conclusion

In this chapter I have argued that experienced professionals, as well as those starting out, can benefit from a mentoring relationship. Communication technologies, such as social networking, can significantly enhance such relationships. Since lack of time is often a reason why mentoring relationships founder, by incorporating technology we can speed up communication and better maintain mentor–mentee contacts. The literature on mentoring and the personal case studies were presented to illustrate how e-mentoring can strengthen and sustain existing relationships.

References

Brockbank, A. and McGill, I. (1998) Mentoring. In A. Brockbank and I. McGill, *Facilitating reflective learning in higher education.* (pp. 252–65). Philadelphia, PA: Society for Research into Higher Education & Open University Press.

Carter, E.M.A. and Caldwell, B.J. (1993) *The Return of the Mentor: Strategies for Workplace Learning.* London; Washington, DC: Falmer Press.

Kem, C.R. (2005) Mentoring: a primer. In P. Schontz (ed.), *The Librarian's Career Guidebook.* Lanham, MD: Scarecrow Press.

Lee, M. (2009) Mentorship in an academic library. *Library Leadership and Management,* 23(1), 31–7.

Muller, C.B. (2009) Understanding e-mentoring in organizations. *Adult Learning,* 20(1/2), 25–30.

Murphy, S. (2008) Developmental relationships in the dynamic library environment: re-conceptualizing mentoring for the future. *The Journal of Academic Librarianship,* 34(5), 434–7.

Nankivell, C. and Shoolbred, M. (1997) Mentoring: a valuable tool for career development. *Librarian Career Development,* 5(3), 98–104.

Newman, B. (2008–10) *A day in the life of a library project.* Retrieved 30 July 2010, from *http://librarydayinthelife .pbworks.com/.*

Ritchie, A. and Genoni, P. (1999). Mentoring in professional associations: continuing professional development for librarians. *Health Libraries Review,* 16, 216–25.

Useful weblinks

ALA New Members Round Table (NMRT): *http://www.ala .org/ala/mgrps/rts/nmrt/oversightgroups/comm/mentor/ mentoringcommittee.cfm*

Australian Library and Information Association (ALIA): *http://www.alia.org.au/education/pd/scheme/*

Canadian Library Association: *http://www.cla.ca/AM/ Template.cfm?Section=Mentoring*

CILIP Mentor Scheme: *http://www.cilip.org.uk/jobs-careers/ qualifications/cilip-qualifications/mentor-scheme/Pages/ default.aspx*

LIANZA Mentoring Manual: *http://www.lianza.org.nz/ resources/professional-registration/mentoring/lianza- mentoring-manual*

LISNPN (LIS New Professionals Network): *http://www .lisnpn.spruz.com/.*

10

Keeping up to date
and being competent

Abstract: This chapter highlights the importance of keeping up to date with professional information in LIS. The chapter discusses the phenomenon of information overload and it provides some strategies to help cope with overload. The chapter focuses on some Web 2.0 technologies, such as blogs, for keeping up to date. It describes social bookmarking and how it can be used as a current awareness tool. The chapter concludes with some discussion of social media competencies for librarians working in the current Web 2.0 environment.

Key words: career, LIS professionals, librarians, Web 2.0, current awareness, information overload, library blogs, social bookmarking, social media competencies.

LIS professionals work at the coalface of the knowledge economy, dealing with growing amounts of information. Describing, organising and making information discoverable is our metier. We help library clients find, evaluate and manage information. Those who work in academic and research libraries are particularly skilled at teaching clients how to set up current awareness alerts, so that they may keep up with information in their discipline. Yet, despite our skills at helping our library clients stay up to date, we may struggle to do so ourselves. At times we may feel that we are overwhelmed and overloaded – drowning in a sea of professional news and information.

In Chapters 6 (on lifelong learning) and 7 (on professional development), I described some ways that professionals can keep up with changes and trends in the LIS field. In this final chapter I focus on how to put our information skills to work and develop strategies for keeping up to date. We all face the dilemma of too much information and not enough time. Whereas keeping up to date is vital, the burgeoning professional literature, from a variety of new sources, can induce stress.

Information overload

Information overload is not a new phenomenon. Over the course of history waves of information production have impacted on individuals and society. The invention of the printing press in the fifteenth century resulted in an explosion of available printed information across Western Europe. By the sixteenth century the scholar Erasmus despaired of keeping up with the printed output and wondered if there was 'anywhere on earth exempt from these swarms of new books' (cited by Blair, 2010). Even further back, in Roman times Seneca complained that 'the abundance of books is a distraction' (cited by Blair, 2010 p. 1). In the 1960s, with the rapid growth in scientific and research publications, the term 'information explosion' was coined (Wikipedia, information explosion) to describe what was happening. In times of rapid change in publishing, information explosions have been perceived as both a blessing and a curse. Nevertheless, the twenty-first-century information overload problem is real and requires effort and a plan to manage it.

Coping with information overload

Sarah Houghton-Jan (2008) has identified the sources of modern-day information overload: RSS, e-mail, phone, interruptive technologies (microblogging and SMS), print media, multimedia and social media. And she has developed some specific time and information management tips to help us cope with information overload:

- Make an inventory of information received.
- Make an inventory of your devices.
- Read up [about information overload and dealing with information generally].
- Think before sending [e-mail, SMS].
- Schedule yourself.
- Schedule unscheduled work.
- Use 'down time' to your benefit.
- Stay tidy and on top.
- Keep a waiting list [daily reminder of the things needing follow up]. (2008)

Houghton-Jan's overall message is that there is a myriad of sources of incoming information that cause overload, and once you have recognised these sources you are on the way to managing them. You then need to take control, prioritise and manage the flow, because the perception that you have lost control induces anxiety. I would add to Houghton-Jan's list above that you must be selective in what information services you sign up for.

How do we take control of information? In reality, no one can keep up with everything and you need to sort out the wheat from the chaff. This requires a combination of time management and information management strategies.

Everyone will approach this differently, and no one way is correct. You need to determine what will work best for you and to not set up unrealistic expectations. For example, some social media experts eschew RSS and advocate Twitter for staying up to date. I prefer a combination of the two, plus some of the Web 2.0 tools described below.

Social media and Web 2.0 technologies offer efficient ways to keep up to date, and they can be incorporated into an overall strategy for managing information. I now describe some of these.

Library and Web 2.0 blogs

Reading blogs is one Web 2.0 way for keeping up to date. Blogs provide current information on library and related areas, such as online education and emerging technologies. Normally, blog posts are concise and written in a style conducive for getting quick updates on topics of current interest. It is not difficult to locate useful library and Web 2.0 blogs. One way is to do a subject search, using blog search tools such as Technorati (*http://technorati.com/*), Google Blog Search (*http://blogsearch.google.com/*), or you can use the blog refining feature on the classic Google advanced search. On these sites you can search for a series of blogs devoted to particular subjects, or individual posts on a particular subject. An excellent source of quality blogs is the annual Edublog awards, which are top blogs that have been shortlisted and voted on (since 2004) to 'promote and demonstrate the educational values of these social media' (*http://edublogawards.com/*). There are now about twenty-three categories of Edublog awards including best individual blog and best librarian/library blog. Because blogs come out irregularly it makes good sense to subscribe to a blog's RSS feed, in the manner I described in Chapter 6.

Library blogs

The library/librarian blogs listed below are a good place to start. Most of them include a 'blogroll' of blogs they follow, which you can use to branch out and find new voices in the blogosphere.

- Abram, Stephen, Stephen's Lighthouse: *http://stephenslighthouse.sirsidynix.com/*
- Australian Libraries Interact (collaborative blog): *http://librariesinteract.info/*
- Bradley, Phil, Phil Bradley's weblog: *http://www.philbradley.typepad.com/*
- Farkas, Meredith, Information wants to be free: *http://meredith.wolfwater.com/wordpress/*
- Greenhill, Kathryn, Librarians Matter: *http://librariansmatter.com/blog/*
- Houghton-Jan, Sarah, Librarian in Black: *http://librarianinblack.net/librarianinblack/*
- Newman, Bobbi, Librarian by Day: *http://librarianbyday.net/*
- Stephens, Michael, Tame the Web: *http://tametheweb.com/*

Web 2.0 and learning technology blogs

Some of the blogs I follow for technology and online learning areas are:

- Brogan, Chris. *http://www.chrisbrogan.com/*
- Mashable. *http://mashable.com/*
- Read Write Web. *http://www.readwriteweb.com/*
- Wheeler, Steve. Learning with 'e's. *http://steve-wheeler.blogspot.com/*

Once you find some useful bloggers, you can explore their other Web 2.0 activities; for example, you can check their social bookmarks (covered below), Twitter feeds and presentations on SlideShare.

SlideShare for staying up to date

Many of the leading professionals in the library and education fields share their presentations on SlideShare (discussed in Chapter 4), which is a social site where members upload and share PowerPoint presentations, Word documents and Adobe PDF presentations. You can follow people on SlideShare to keep up with new presentations (see Figure 10.1).

Some of the leading names in the LIS and related fields are:

- Karen Blakeman: *http://www.slideshare.net/KarenBlakeman*
- Helene Blowers: *http://www.slideshare.net/hblowers*

Figure 10.1   Example of a SlideShare page

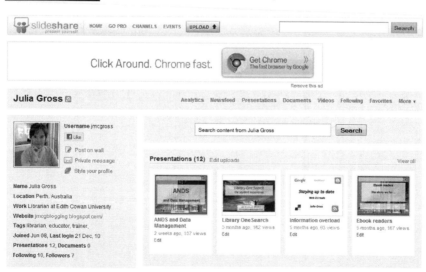

- Meredith Farkas: *http://www.slideshare.net/librarianmer*
- Sarah Houghton-Jan: *http://www.slideshare.net/librarian inblack*
- Steve Wheeler: *http://www.slideshare.net/timbuckteeth*

As I have mentioned previously, some conference papers appear on SlideShare before they are posted on the conference website. Depending on how copyright has been assigned, some SlideShare presentation slides can be reused (with acknowledgment) under a Creative Commons licence. The presentations on the SlideShare site will include this information, so look out for it. Creative Commons is a 'nonprofit corporation dedicated to making it easier for people to share and build upon the work of others, consistent with the rules of copyright' (*http://creativecommons.org/about*).

RSS for staying up to date

I discussed RSS feeds and feed readers in Chapter 6. Alerts from LIS professional journals (for table of contents and topics) and from LIS monograph publishers (for new titles) can be set up to come to you via e-mail or RSS. RSS is the key Web 2.0 way to stay up to date, but it can contribute to information overload and must be well managed.

Tips for better use of RSS:

- Be very selective in choosing your RSS subscriptions.
- Delete old feeds when your interests change.
- Tag and describe feeds in your feed reader (for example Google Reader).
- Group your feeds into subject folders.
- Organise feeds into a functional workspace (for example within a start page, as was described in Chapter 6).

RSS should contribute to controlling your information load, rather than adding to it, but it does need to be set up correctly, as I have shown.

Twitter for staying up to date

Twitter provides news and updates in an engaging way. I use Twitter as a current awareness tool as well as RSS. However, I know some people find there is too much trivia on Twitter for it to be of benefit for keeping up. One effective way to get current awareness updates on particular topics via Twitter is to follow a topic hash tag. Hash tags are assigned by users of Twitter to cover events, conferences and topics, which I described in some detail in Chapter 3.

However, Twitter can become overwhelming and contribute to overload. One way to control this is to use a Twitter client (application software), such as Tweetdeck, to manage and group incoming Twitter messages into lists. Make some lists of the top priority people you follow; others could be the ones you get to when you have spare time. Different Twitter clients include different management tools. The Twitter native interface is adding enhancements all the time and you can now create lists to group people together according to topic or interest. Approach your management of Twitter in the same way as you would with RSS.

These are some tips for better management of Twitter as a professional tool:

- Be selective in choosing who you follow.
- Before following someone, check out their profile, including links to their blog or website, to see how relevant the content is.

- cease following someone when you see no value;
- unless critical, do not go back over Twitter messages you have missed – this can be time consuming and fruitless;
- use Twitter's search function if you need to locate a past tweet;
- check out the Twitter hash tags people assign to their tweets to see what is relevant;
- organise tweets into subject groups and/or people groups, using the functions in Twitter or your Twitter client.

Social bookmarking

Social bookmarking sites assist you to keep track of the mountains of links you come across on the web. To conceptualise social bookmarking, think of it as a Web 2.0 technology that creates a database of all your bookmarks and/or favourites. The bookmarks could be links to websites, blogs, blog posts, news, reports, conference papers, PDFs, journal articles or anything on the open web.

Social bookmarking solves the problem of keeping track of all your web browser bookmarks. If you use many different browsers, or use different computers at work and at home, you may find that your browser bookmarks are scattered across different computers.

There are four functions in social bookmarking:

- storing bookmarks
- describing bookmarks
- organising bookmarks
- sharing bookmarks.

A description of each of these functions follows.

Storing bookmarks

There are several sites where you can store your bookmarks or favourites on the web, so that wherever you are and whatever browser you are using, you will be able to access your bookmarks. The most popular social bookmarking site over the past few years has been Delicious (*http://www .delicious.com/*), which is owned by Yahoo! However, in December 2010 Yahoo! announced that they were planning to sell Delicious, so there may be changes in the future. Another site is Diigo (*http://www.diigo.com*), which has more functionality than Delicious and allows you to store bookmarks, highlighted text, sticky notes, images and links within tweets. Both sites offer toolbar button downloads for all the major web browsers and it is far more efficient in the long run to install the browser buttons onto your browser toolbar.

Describing (tagging) bookmarks

The key to unlocking the potential of social bookmarking is to effectively describe your bookmarked links at the point when you save them on Delicious or Diigo. You do this by tagging each bookmark. When you save a bookmark to Delicious or Diigo the system offers you the option to tag (assign keywords) and add some personal notes and a description of each link. Tags are similar to keywords and they provide the metadata that is crucial for later retrieval.

Note that tags should be entered as one word without any commas. Multi-word phrases must be linked together to form one word. So, for example, the two words 'career development' would become the tag: 'career_development' or 'careerdevelopment' or other one-word combinations.

It does not matter how you combine multiple terms, but do not leave them as separate words, or the system will make separate tags out of them. There is no limit to the number of tags you can add for each bookmark, so use the tagging function liberally. The true librarian in you will relish the describing and organising aspect of social bookmarking. Be quite thorough at this stage – a disorganised social book-marking account will only confuse you when you go back in later. The time spent tagging bookmarks at the outset will save you time later. What tag should you use? You may have your own schema that you use for other Web 2.0 sites. Try to be systematic here so you do not have to do a clean-up later. However, on both Delicious and Diigo you can go back and edit your saved bookmarks and add new tags and descriptions later if you wish. This method of making up your own tags is known as a folksonomy and is not meant to be perfect. Folksonomies are systems 'of classification derived from the practice and method of collaboratively creating and mana-ging tags to annotate and categorize content' (Wikipedia, folksonomy definition). Once you have a number of tagged bookmarks in your social bookmarking account, start to organise them into groups or lists.

Organising bookmarks

Organise your bookmarks by grouping them together in folders. Delicious calls these groupings 'tag bundles' and Diigo calls them lists. There is no particular need to place all tags in bundles or lists, but the bundles and lists are useful for larger subject areas that you may be researching. Both websites offer help and advice on the organising of bookmarks: Delicious (*http://www.delicious.com/help*) and Diigo (*http://help.diigo.com/*).

Sharing bookmarks

Bookmarking can be a shared activity, hence the name social bookmarking. Once you have saved a bookmark, you can see how many others have saved it. If users have an open account, as most do, you can link through to see what other bookmarks that person has saved. On both Delicious and Diigo you can set up networks of like-minded colleagues. Social bookmarking is largely a self development and professional development tool. I personally find it one of the most useful Web 2.0 ways for keeping up and managing the online information I come across on a daily basis.

Tag or word clouds

Tag clouds or word clouds (see Figure 10.2) are popular ways to visually represent tags giving them a weighting based on the frequency of a word in a given piece of text. Some social bookmarking sites allow you to make tag clouds from your own tags. The word cloud below has been created from all the tags I have used on Delicious, the social bookmarking site. What this shows is the most common tag I have used to describe my bookmarks is 'Web 2.0' as this appears in the largest text. This is followed by 'socialnetworking' and so forth. A tag cloud can show you what words you commonly use in a piece of text and where your overall interests lie.

The word or tag cloud above has been generated from the Wordle website: *http://www.wordle.net/*. Wordle is a free site where you can create a word cloud based on a piece of text, a blog, a site that has RSS feeds, or a Delicious user name. The Wordle site offers many word cloud options in various fonts, colours and layouts.

Figure 10.2   Wordle.net tag cloud from Del.icio.us tags

Housekeeping and keeping track of passwords

I have covered many social software sites throughout the book: Facebook, Twitter, LinkedIn and SlideShare to name a few. As you delve into social media and Web 2.0 and create accounts, it is easy to lose track of your multiple logins and passwords. To complicate matters, experts say that to be secure online you need to have a different password on each site. Managing your different accounts is sound practice and helps you stay of top of things. The 'social-i.net' blog has some advice on how to manage passwords: *http://social-i .net/wordpress-2.9.2/wordpress/?p=15*. Their advice is to:

- maintain a record of the online accounts and profiles you already have;
- choose a secure password that is not a dictionary word;
- have different passwords for each site;
- use password management software to keep a record.

Some password management software packages are Passpack (*http://www.passpack.com/en/home/*) and eWallet (*http:// www.iliumsoft.com/site/ew/ewallet.php*).

Having an efficient method for managing the information flows and attending to logins and profiles will help to avoid overload, and help you to keep up to date in the long run.

Social media competencies for LIS professionals

Of the technologies I have covered in this book, many will evolve over time, some will become obsolete, and others will disappear altogether. So we need to recognise that our focus in the long term should be not on the technologies per se, but on Web 2.0 competencies. Along with the particular Web 2.0 tools that have been described throughout the book, there is an associated set of competencies that come with the active use and understanding of Web 2.0 and social media. Some LIS researchers (Murphy and Moulaison, 2009; Guistini, 2010) are advocating that 'social media competencies' be recognised as a new set of literacies required for librarians who work in the Web 2.0 environment. A draft list of these social media competencies is set out below:

- Understand, explain and teach others about the main principles and trends of Web 2.0 (and Library 2.0).
- List major tools, categories and affordances of social networking.
- Apply social media to solve information problems, and communicate digitally with users.
- Use social networking sites for promotional, reference and instructional services in libraries.
- Navigate, evaluate and create content on social networking sites.
- Follow netiquette, conform to ethical standards, and interact appropriately with others online.

- Explain copyright, security and privacy issues on social media sites to colleagues and user communities.

- Understand the importance of identity and reputation management using social media.

- Explain related terminology such as collaboration 2.0, remix and open source.

- Renew social media competencies, advocate for institutional strategies and policies, and build an evidence base in social media. (Giustini, 2010)

In the paper Murphy and Moulaison (2009) presented at the Association of College and Research Libraries (ACRL) they have fully described these competencies and related them back to the established ACRL information literacy competencies. Whether or not these new competencies gain acceptance by the profession at large, they serve as goals that LIS professionals should be aiming towards to broaden the skill base. They also alert us to the continuing importance of Web 2.0 and social media for the future of the profession. Murphy and Moulaison are advocating that we go beyond just gaining knowledge of how to use particular Web 2.0 technologies to gain an understanding of the changing information landscape in which librarians operate.

In this book I have covered many of these social media competency areas: Chapters 2 and 3 dealt with creating content on social networking sites, Chapter 4 with identity and reputation management, Chapter 5 with privacy, and Chapters 5, 6, 7, 8, 9 and 10 with applying social media to learning, networking and career development.

Conclusion

Building your library career with Web 2.0 entails developing new competencies and looking for learning and networking opportunities within and without the library and information services area. One of the exciting aspects of the digital world is the core idea of convergence. The walls between disciplines are coming down, and colleagues in communications, online learning and digital media are experiencing the same trends and influences that are shaping libraries. Web 2.0 provides you with the means to share and collaborate across sectors, grow professionally and develop your career. I wish you well in pursuing these goals.

References

Blair, A. (2010) *Information overload, the early years, The Boston Globe*. Retrieved 8 December 2010, from *http:// www.boston.com/bostonglobe/ideas/articles/2010/11/28/ information_overload_the_early_years/*.

Giustini, D. (2010) *Top ten (10) social media competencies for librarians. The Search principle blog*. Retrieved 6 October 2010, from *http://blogs.ubc.ca/dean/2010/07/ top-ten-10-social-media-competencies-for-librarians/*.

Houghton-Jan, S. (2008) *Being wired or being tired: 10 ways to cope with information overload. Ariadne, 56*. Retrieved 24 October 2010, from *http://www.ariadne .ac.uk/issue56/houghton-jan*.

Murphy, J. and Moulaison, H. (2009) *Social networking literacy competencies for librarians: exploring considerations and engaging participation*. Paper presented at the ACRL 14th National Conference, Pushing the Edge: Explore, Engage, Extend. Seattle, WA. Retrieved 24 October 2010, from *http://eprints.rclis.org/16219/1/ Social_networking_Literacy_for_librarians.pdf*.

Useful weblinks

100 Best Blogs for Librarians of the Future: *http://www .bachelorsdegreeonline.com/blog/2009/100-best-blogs- for-librarians-of-the-future/*

Creative Commons: *http://creativecommons.org/about*

Del.icio.us: *http://del.icio.us* or *www.delicious.com*

Diigo: *http://www.diigo.com/index*

Edublog awards 2004–10: *http://edublogawards.com/*

eWallet (password management): *http://www.iliumsoft.com/ site/ew/ewallet.php*

Google Blog Search: *http://blogsearch.google.com/*

Passpack (password management): *http://www.passpack .com/en/home/*

SlideShare: *http://www.slideshare.net/*

Social-i.net blog. The Social blog. Managing your online life and password security: *http://social-i.net/wordpress-2.9.2/ wordpress/?p=15*

Technorati: *http://technorati.com/*

Wikipedia. Folksonomy (definition): *http://en.wikipedia.org/ wiki/Folksonomy*

Wikipedia. Information_explosion (definition): *http://en .wikipedia.org/wiki/Information_explosion*

Wordle.net: *http://www.wordle.net/*

Bibliography

Abelson, H., Ledeen, K. and Lewis, H. (2008) *Blown to Bits: Your Life, Liberty, and Happiness.* Upper Saddle River, NJ: Addison-Wesley.

Abram, S. (2007) *The Future of Libraries.* Retrieved 20 May 2008, from *http://stephenslighthouse.com/files/Monterey PL.pdf.*

Allen, T.D. and Eby, L.T. (2007) *The Blackwell Handbook of Mentoring: a Multiple Perspectives Approach.* Malden, MA and Oxford: Blackwell Publishing.

Anderson, J. and Rainie, L. (2010) *Millennials will make online sharing in networks a lifelong habit.* Pew Internet & American Life Project, 9 July 2010. Retrieved 1 August 2010, from *http://pewinternet.org/Reports/2010/Future-of-Millennials.aspx.*

Anderson, P. (2007) *What is Web 2.0? Ideas, technologies and implications for education. TechWatch report.* Retrieved 5 March 2008, from *http://www.jisc.ac.uk/publications/browsetypes/reports.aspx.*

Arruda, W. and Dixson, K. (2007) *Career Distinction: Stand Out by Building your Brand.* Hoboken, NJ: J. Wiley & Sons.

Atlay, M. and Harris, R. (2000) An institutional approach to developing students' transferable skills. *Innovations in Education and Training International,* 37(1), 76–84.

Bates, M.E. (2003) Marketing on the web. In M.E. Bates and R. Basch, *Building & running a successful research business: a guide for the independent information professional* (pp. 245–57). Medford, NJ: CyberAge Books.

Bates, M.E. (2010) *Brand you and Web 2.0*. Paper presented at the SLA Annual Conference, New Orleans, USA. Retrieved 5 November 2010, from *http://www.batesinfo.com/extras/index_assets/SLA-Brand-You.pdf*.

Bennett, T. and Wiebrands, C. (2010) *Out on the edge: using a personal learning network for continuing professional development*. Paper presented at the ALIA Access 2010, Brisbane, Australia. Retrieved 2 December 2010, from *http://conferences.alia.org.au/access2010/pdf/ Paper_Thu_1410_Teresa_Bennett.pdf*.

Betancourt, L. (2009) *Protecting online identity. Mashable.* Retrieved 25 August 2010, from *http://mashable.com/ 2009/04/21/protecting-online-identity/*.

Blair, A. (2010) *Information overload, the early years, The Boston Globe*. Retrieved 30 November 2010, from *http://www.boston.com/bostonglobe/ideas/articles/ 2010/11/28/information_overload_the_early_years/*.

Bloch, D.P. (2004) The Living career: complexity, chaos, connections and career. In G.R. Walz and R.L. Knowdell (eds), *Global realities* (pp. 219–27). Greensboro, NC: CAPS Press.

Blowers, H. (2006) *Learning 2.0* (blog). Retrieved 1 March 2007, from *http://plcmclearning.blogspot.com/*.

boyd, d. (2008) Facebook's privacy trainwreck: Exposure, invasion, and social convergence. *Convergence,* 14(1).

boyd, d. (2010) *Public by default, private when necessary*. Retrieved 5 July 2010 from *http://www.zephoria .org/thoughts/archives/2010/01/25/public_by_defau .html*.

boyd, d. and Hargittai, E. (2010) Facebook privacy settings: Who cares? *First Monday,* 15(8).

Bozarth, J. (2010) *Social media for trainers: Techniques for enhancing and extending learning.* Hoboken, NJ: John Wiley & Sons.

Bradley, P. (2007) *How to use Web 2.0 in your library.* London: Facet Publishing.

Bradley, P. (2009) *Twitter.* Retrieved 1 March 2010, from *http://www.philb.com/twitter.htm.*

Breeding, M. (2009) Social networking strategies for professionals. *Computers in libraries,* 29(9), 29–31.

Brine, A. (2005) *Continuing professional development: a guide for information professionals.* Oxford: Chandos.

Brockbank, A. and McGill, I. (1998) Mentoring. In A. Brockbank and I. McGill, *Facilitating reflective learning in higher education* (pp. 252–65). Philadelphia, PA: Society for Research into Higher Education and Open University Press.

Brown, R. (2009) *Public relations and the social web: How to use social media and Web 2.0 in communications.* London: Kogan Page.

Carruthers, K. (2010) *Digital revolution not going away. Aide memoire* (blog). Retrieved 4 September 2010, from *http://katecarruthers.com/blog/2010/06/digital-revolution-not-going-away/.*

Carter, E.M.A. and Caldwell, B.J. (1993) *The Return of the Mentor: Strategies for Workplace Learning.* London and Washington, DC: Falmer Press.

CCH (2008) Professionals and Web 2.0: Findings from the CCH whitepaper and what it means for information providers. Retrieved 20 April 2010, from *http://www.cch.com.au/DocLibrary/cch_professionals_web20_whitepaper_final.pdf.*

Charnigo, L. and Barnett-Ellis, P. (2007) Checking out Facebook.com: The Impact of a digital trend on academic libraries. *Information Technology and Libraries,* 26(1), 23.

Chu, M. and Meulemans, Y.N. (2008) The problems and potential of MySpace and Facebook usage in academic libraries. *Internet Reference Services Quarterly*, 13(1), 69–85.

Clyde, L.A. (2004) *Weblogs and Libraries*. Oxford: Chandos.

Cook, N. (2008) *Enterprise 2.0: How Social Software will Change the Future of Work*. Aldershot, England; Burlington, VT: Gower.

Cook, S. and Wiebrands, C. (2010) *Keeping up: strategic use of online social networks for librarian current awareness*. Paper presented at the VALA2010: connections, content, conversations. 15th Biennial Conference and exhibition, Melbourne, Australia. Retrieved 7 September 2010, from *http://www.vala.org.au/vala2010/papers2010/ VALA2010_78_Cook_Final.pdf*.

Cummings, D. and Tairi, K. (2009) *Walking on clouds: managing your digital footprints*. Paper presented at the EDUCAUSE Australasia, Perth, Western Australia. Retrieved 7 July, 2009, from *http://www.caudit.edu.au/ educauseaustralasia09/*.

De Sáez, E.E. (2002) *Marketing Concepts for Libraries and Information Services* (2nd edn). London: Facet Publishing.

De Stricker, U. and Hurst-Wahl, J. (2011) *The Information and Knowledge Professional's Career Handbook: Define and Create your Success*. Oxford: Chandos.

Dority, K.G. (2006) *Rethinking Information Work: A Career Guide for Librarians and Other Information Professionals*. Westport, CN: Libraries Unlimited.

Dority, K.G. (2010) *Infonista: on being and information entrepreneur* (blog). Retrieved 1 September 2010, from *http://infonista.com/2010/discussions-list-linkedin-lis-career-options-group/*.

Dougherty, H. (2010) *Facebook reached top ranking.* Retrieved 2 July 2010, from *http://weblogs.hitwise.com/ heather-dougherty/2010/03/facebook_reaches_top_ ranking_i.html.*

Duffy, J. (2009) *Tweeted out of a job: the 'Cisco Fatty' story. Networkworld* (blog). Retrieved 15 September 2010, from *http://www.networkworld.com/community/node/39874.*

Elad, J. (2011) *LinkedIn for Dummies* (2nd edn). Hoboken, NJ: John Wiley & Sons.

Farkas, M.G. (2007) *Social software in libraries: building collaboration, communication, and community online.* Medford, NJ: Information Today.

Fletcher, D. (2010) How Facebook is redefining privacy. *Time,* 175(21), 1.

Foo, F. (2010) *Google Australia breached Privacy Act with Street View but escapes with apology. The Australian.* Retrieved 2 August 2010, from *http://www .theaustralian.com.au/australian-it/google-australia- breached-privacy-act-but-apology-is-sufficient/story-e6 frgakx-1225889876666.*

Forsyth, F. (2008) *Framing your digital footprint. Conference keynote.* Paper presented at the EDNA Conference, Adelaide, South Australia. Retrieved 7 July 2009, from *http://www.slideshare.net/frankie/keynote-edna-july- 2008.*

Giustini, D. (2010) *Top ten (10) social media competencies for librarians. The Search principle blog.* Retrieved 6 October 2010, from *http://blogs.ubc.ca/dean/2010/07/ top-ten-10-social media-competencies-for-librarians/.*

Gordon, R.S. (2006) *The Nextgen Librarian's Survival Guide.* Medford, NJ: Information Today.

Grant, S. (2009) *Electronic Portfolios: Personal Information, Personal Development and Personal Values.* Oxford: Chandos.

Gray, L. (2008) *Effective practice with e-portfolios supporting 21st century learning*. Retrieved 7 September 2010, from *http://www.jisc.ac.uk/media/documents/publications/ effectivepracticeeportfolios.pdf.*

Greenhill, K. and Wiebrands, C. (2008) *The unconference: a new model for better professional communication.* Paper presented at the Poropitia outside the box: LIANZA Conference, Auckland, New Zealand. Retrieved 7 September 2010, from *http://opac.lianza.org.nz/cgi-bin/koha/opac-detail.pl?bib=383.*

Gross, J. and Leslie, L. (2008) Twenty-three steps to learning Web 2.0 technologies in an academic library *The Electronic Library,* 26(6), 790–802.

Haefner, R. and CareerBuilder (2009, 6 October) *More employers screening candidates via social networking sites: Five tips for creating a positive online image.* Retrieved 20 April 2010, from *http://msn.careerbuilder.com/Article/ MSN-2035-Job-Info-and-Trends-More-Employers-Screening-Candidates-via-Social-Networking-Sites/.*

Hallam, G.C. and McAllister, L.M. (2008) *Self discovery through digital portfolios: a holistic approach to developing new library and information professionals.* Paper presented at the Digital discovery: strategies and solutions: 29th Annual Conference of the International Association of Technological University Libraries (IATUL), Auckland, New Zealand. Retrieved 7 June 2010, from *http://eprints .qut.edu.au/14048/1/14048.pdf.*

Hallam, G.C. and Newton-Smith, C. (2006) Evaluation of transitional mentoring for new library and information professionals. *Library Management,* 27(3), 154–67.

Heye, D. (2006) *Characteristics of the Successful Twenty-first Century Information Professional.* Oxford: Chandos.

Hills, C., Randle, R. and Beazley, J. (2010) *ePortfolios a plan for success: Australian new graduate experiences.* Paper presented at the IFLA 2010 Open access to knowledge – promoting sustainable progress, Gothenburg, Sweden. Retrieved 7 December 2010, from *http://www/ifla.org/en/ifla76*.

Houghton-Jan, S. (2008) *Being wired or being tired: 10 ways to cope with information overload. Ariadne, 56*. Retrieved 24 October 2010, from *http://www.ariadne.ac.uk/issue56/houghton-jan*.

Hurst-Wahl, J. (2010) *eNetworking 101: Helping you build & extend your network with social networking tools* (blog). Retrieved 2 November 2010, from *http://enetworking 101.blogspot.com/*.

Jafari, A. and Kaufman, C. (2006) *Handbook of Research on ePortfolios*. Hershey, PA: Idea Group Reference.

Kawasaki, G. (2007) *Ten ways to use LinkedIn*. Retrieved 2 September 2010, from *http://blog.guy kawasaki.com/2007/01/ten_ways_to_use.html#axzz0tSSs FG9b*.

Kem, C.R. (2005) Mentoring: a primer. In P. Schontz (Ed.), *The Librarian's Career Guidebook*. Lanham, MD: Scarecrow Press.

Kirkpatrick, D. (2010) *The Facebook Effect: the Inside Story of the Company that is Connecting the World*. New York: Simon & Schuster.

Kirkpatrick, M. (2010) *Facebook's Zuckerberg says the age of privacy is over. Read Write Web* (blog). Retrieved 23 August 2011, from *http://www.readwriteweb.com/archives/facebooks_zuckerberg_says_the_age_of_privacy_is_ov.php*.

Knowles, M.S. (1990) *The Adult learner: a neglected species* (4th edn). Houston, TX: Gulf.

Kolb, D.A. (1984) *Experiential learning: experience as the source of learning and development*. Englewood Cliffs, NJ: Prentice-Hall.

Kujawski, M. (2009) *Latest mobile phone statistics from Africa and what this means.* Retrieved 1 July, 2010, from *http://www.mikekujawski.ca/2009/03/16/latest-mobile-phone-statistics-from-africa-and-what-this-means/.*

Lee, M. (2009) Mentorship in an academic library. *Library leadership and management,* 23(1), 31–7.

Leslie, S. and Langdon, B. (2008) Social software for learning: what it is, why use it? London: The Observatory on Borderless Higher Education.

LIScareer.com. (2000–10) *Career strategies for librarians.* Retrieved 21 October 2010, from *http://www.liscareer.com/.*

Longworth, N. and Davies, W.K. (1996) *Lifelong Learning: New Vision, New Implications, New Roles for People, Organizations, Nations and Communities in the 21st Century.* London: Kogan Page.

Lorenzo, G. and Ittelson, J. (2005) *An overview of e-portfolios. Educause.* Retrieved 2 December 2010 from *http://net.educause.edu/ir/library/pdf/ELI3001.pdf.*

MacLennan, B. (2004) Staying relevant: It's all part of learning. In P. Schontz (Ed.), *The Librarian's Career Guidebook* (pp. 312–24). Lanham, MD: Scarecrow Press.

MacManus, R. and Kirkpatrick, M. (2010) *ReadWriteWeb* (blog). *ReadWriteWeb.* Retrieved 8 June 2010, from *http://www.readwriteweb.com/.*

Madden, M. and Smith, A. (2010) *Reputation management and social media: How people monitor their identity and search for others online.* Pew Internet & American Life Project, 26 May 2010. Retrieved 13 September 2010, from *http://www.pewinternet.org/Reports/2010/Reputation-Management.aspx.*

Maehl, W.H. (2003) Lifelong Learning. In J. W. Guthrie (ed.), *Encyclopedia of education* (2nd edn., Vol. 4, pp. 1480–3). New York: Macmillan Reference USA.

Maness, J.M. (2006) *Library 2.0 theory: Web 2.0 and its implications for libraries. Webology,* 3(2), Article 25. Retrieved 4 May 2010, from *http://www.webology.ir/2006/v3n2/a25.html.*

Markgren, S. (2010) *Using portfolios and profiles to professionalize your online identity (for free).* Retrieved 2 December 2010, from *http://www.liscareer.com/markgren_portfolio.htm.*

McKnight, M. (2010) *The Agile librarian's guide to thriving in any institution.* Santa Barbara, CA: Libraries Unlimited.

Mejias, U. (2005) *A nomad's guide to learning and social software.* Retrieved 22 May 2010, from *http://knowledgetree.flexiblelearning.net.au/edition07/download/la_mejias.pdf.*

Miller, P. (2006) *Library 2.0: The challenge of disruptive innovation. A TALIS White Paper.* Retrieved 4 March 2008, from *http://www.talis.com/tdn/node/1304.*

Morris, T. (2010) *All a twitter: a personal and professional guide to social networking with Twitter.* Indianapolis, IN: Que.

Morton, A. (2003) *Mentoring. Continuing professional development series 2.* Retrieved 22 March 2007, from *http://www.kent.ac.uk/uelt/staff_development/pgche/ltsnmentoring_annmorton.pdf.*

Muller, C.B. (2009) Understanding e-mentoring in organizations. *Adult Learning,* 20(1/2), 25–30.

Murphy, J. and Moulaison, H. (2009) *Social networking literacy competencies for librarians: exploring considerations and engaging participation.* Paper presented at the ACRL 14th National Conference, Pushing the Edge: Explore, Engage, Extend. Seattle, WA. Retrieved 7 September 2010, from *http://eprints.rclis.org/16219/1/Social_networking_Literacy_for_librarians.pdf.*

Murphy, S. (2008) Developmental relationships in the dynamic library environment: re-conceptualizing mentoring for the future. *The Journal of Academic Librarianship*, 34(5), 434–7.

Myburgh, S. (2005) *The New Information Professional: How to Thrive in the Information Age Doing What You Love*. Oxford: Chandos.

Nankivell, C. and Shoolbred, M. (1997) Mentoring: a valuable tool for career development. *Librarian Career Development*, 5(3), 98–104.

Newman, B. (2008–10) *A day in the life of a library project* (wiki). Retrieved 30 July, 2010, from *http://librarydayinthe life.pbworks.com/*.

OCLC. (2007) *Sharing, privacy and trust in our networked world: A Report to the OCLC membership*. Dublin, OH: OCLC.

Pantry, S. and Griffiths, P. (2003) *Your essential guide to career success* (2nd edn). London: Facet Publishing.

Park, J-H. (2010) Differences among university students and faculties in social networking site perception and use. *Implications for academic library services*, 28(3), 417.

Privacy, schmivacy: Facebook is attracting near-record numbers of new visitors (2010) *TechCrunch* (blog). Retrieved 25 August 2010, from *http://techcrunch.com/2010/06/07/ privacy-facebook-visitors/*.

Ptolomey, J. (2009) *Taking Charge of Your Career: a Guide for the Library and Information Professional*. Oxford: Chandos.

Ritchie, A. and Genoni, P. (1999) Mentoring in professional associations: continuing professional development for librarians. *Health Libraries Review,* 16, 216–25.

Ross, C., Terras, M., Warwick, C. and Welsh, A. (2011) Enabled backchannel: Conference Twitter use by digital humanists. *Journal of Documentation,* 67(2).

Rossiter, N. (2008) *Marketing the Best Deal in Town: Your Library: Where is Your Purple Owl?* Oxford: Chandos.

Rutledge, P.A. (2010) *Using LinkedIn.* Indianapolis, IN: Que.

Saunders, L. (2003) Professional portfolios for librarians. *College and undergraduate libraries,* 10(1), 53–9.

Shontz, P. (2002) *Why network?* Retrieved 2 November 2010, from *http://www.liscareer.com/shontz_networking.htm.*

Shontz, P. (ed.). (2004) *The Librarian's Career Guidebook.* Lanham, MD: Scarecrow Press.

Shumaker, D. (2010) *The embedded librarian* (blog). Retrieved 10 October 2010, from *http://embeddedlibrarian.wordpress.com.*

Siemens, G. (2005) *Connectivism: a Learning theory for the digital age. International Journal of Instructional Technology and Distance Learning,* 2(1). Retrieved 10 October 2010, from *http://www.itdl.org/Journal/Jan_05/article01.htm.*

Stefani, L., Mason, R. and Pegler, C. (2007) *The Educational Potential of e-Portfolios: Supporting Personal Development and Reflective Learning.* Abingdon, Oxon. and New York, NY: Routledge.

Steiner, P. (1993) On the Internet, nobody knows you're a dog (cartoon), *New Yorker* p. 61.

Stephens, M. (2007) *Tools from 'web 2.0 and libraries: best practices for social software' revisited. Library Technology Reports.* Retrieved 2 July 2010, from *http://alatechsource.metapress.com/content/u1086q436601l068/fulltext.pdf.*

Stephenson, K. (1998) *What knowledge tears apart, networks make whole. Internal Communication Focus no. 36.* Retrieved 2 November 2010, *from http://www.netform.com/html/icf.pdf.*

Telegraph.co.uk. (2010) *Top 10 gaffes on Facebook, Twitter and Google*. Retrieved 15 September 2010, from *http:// www.telegraph.co.uk/technology/facebook/7635982/ Top-10-gaffes-on-Facebook-Twitter-and-Google.html*.

University of Cambridge Library. (2010) *23 Things Cambridge blog*. Retrieved 22 October 2010, from *http://23 thingscambridge.blogspot.com/2010*.

Waters, S. (2010) *A Twitteraholics guide to tweets hashtags and all things Twitter*. Retrieved 2 September 2010, from *http://theedublogger.com/2010/07/08/a-twitteraholics-guide-to-tweets-hashtags-and-all-things-twitter/*.

Webb, J., Gannon-Leary, P. and Bent, M. (2007) *Providing Effective Library Services for Research*. London: Facet Publishing.

Weinberg, T. (2008) *Manage your online reputation. Lifehacker*. Retrieved 25 August 2010, from *http://lifehacker .com/357460/manage-your-online-reputation*.

Wheeler, S. (2010) *I store my knowledge with my friends. Learning with 'e's* (blog). Retrieved 1 November 2010, from *http://steve-wheeler.blogspot.com/2010/10/i-store-my-knowledge-with-my-friends.html*.

Index

05803679